ANCIENT HEALING SECRETS

ANCIENT HEALING SECRETS

PRACTICAL CURES THAT WORK TODAY

DIAN DINCIN BUCHMAN, PH.D.

Ottenheimer Publishers, Inc.

Published by Ottenheimer Publishers, Inc.
5 Park Center Court, Suite 300
Owings Mills, Maryland 21117
Printed in the United States of America
SH115L

Dedicated to my loving daughter,
Caitlin Dincin Kraft Buchman

NOTE TO THE READER

The information in *Ancient Healing Secrets* is designed to help increase your knowledge of traditional remedies that may relieve health problems in some cases. This book is intended as a reference resource only, and does not purport to give medical advice. Do not use any remedy in this book without first consulting your physician or in place of prompt and proper medical care. The information contained in this book is not intended to substitute for the advice of your physician or any treatment that he or she may prescribe or recommend. Instead, use this book as a complement to your cooperative relationship with your physician.

TABLE OF CONTENTS

Introduction viii
How Herbs Were Prepared ix
A Guide to Symbols xi
Acne 1
Acute Pain 3
Age Spots 6
Anxiety 9
Arthritis 12
Asthma 15
Athlete's Foot 17
Back Pain 19
Boils 21
Bone Regeneration 24
Bruises 25
Burns 27
Cavities 29
Chills 31
Colds 33
Constipation 39
Corns and Calluses 43
Coughs 45
Cuts and Wounds 47
Cystitis 49
Depression 52
Diarrhea 55
Ear Infections 57
Edema 59
Eye Problems 61
Fatigue 64
Fever 66

Flatulence . . . 70
Foot Pain . . . 73
Frostbite . . . 75
Gum Disease . . . 78
Hair Loss . . . 81
Hay Fever . . . 84
Headaches . . . 86
Heartburn . . . 91
Heart Palpitations . . . 93
Heat Exhaustion . . . 95
Hemorrhoids . . . 99
Hiccups . . . 103
High Blood Pressure . . . 107
Hoarseness . . . 110
Incontinence . . . 112
Infections . . . 115
Inflammation . . . 118
Influenza . . . 122
Insect Bites . . . 124
Insomnia . . . 127
Irregular Periods . . . 129
Memory Loss . . . 133
Muscle Spasms/Cramps . . . 136
Nasal and Sinus Congestion . . . 139
Nausea . . . 142
Nosebleeds . . . 144
Rashes . . . 147
Sore Throats . . . 151
Sprains . . . 154
Tooth Sensitivity . . . 156
Vaginal Infections . . . 159
Vision Problems . . . 164
Warts . . . 166
Wrinkles/Aging Problems . . . 168
Appendix I—Mail-order Sources . . . 173
Appendix II—Natural Health Practitioner Organizations . . . 175
About the Author . . . 176

INTRODUCTION

In the earliest times cures worked mostly by chance. The ancients may not have understood why a remedy worked, but once it did, they repeated that cure. Eventually, every culture accumulated a vast historical and cultural sourcebook of proven cures. As Herodotus, the Greek historian, describes medicine in the ancient civilization of Babylonia:

> They bring out the sick to the market place, for they do not use physicians. People walk by, and those who have suffered the same ill as the sick man's or seen others in like case, come near and advise him about his disease and comfort him, telling him by what means they have recovered of it, or seen others to recover. None may pass by the sick man without speaking and asking what is his sickness.

Ancient Healing Secrets is a journey into antiquity to recapture some of the safe and practical healing remedies of the past and to adapt them to the needs of modern men and women.

The ancients were keen observers. A 4,000-year-old Sumerian clay tablet, one of the oldest medical manuscripts in the world, shows a series of astonishingly modern procedures: wounds were first washed with a kind of liquid soap made of beer and water, poultices or plasters applied, and finally bandages. In today's laboratories, time and again scientists find that ancient herbs used to treat wounds are usually effective against staphylococcus or *E. coli* bacteria, or both. Egyptians used honey in most of their wound recipes. Why? Current researchers discovered that honey breaks down to a common household disinfectant, hydrogen peroxide. In 1536, French explorer Cartier's party was saved from scurvy by the Canadian Iroquois who showed the Europeans how to make a vitamin C drink with either hemlock or white pine needles. At that time the Iroquois exceeded even European surgeons' skill at healing wounds and setting fractures. Amputations were cauterized with an ember wrapped in a leaf of Indian corn and left in a poultice made of roots or barks.

In 1865, Dr. Joseph Lister revolutionized surgery with the sterilization of instruments and by using carbolic acid, a simple phenol, as an antiseptic. If only surgeons before his time had known the practices of the early Greeks. They washed the wounds of the sick with red wine, a powerful antiseptic and a complex *poly*-phenol. Modern chemists seeking an anti-inflammatory drug took their inspiration for aspirin from the African and Native American use of the willow tree. Over four thousand years ago, the Egyptians applied rotten moldy bread to control infected wounds; it took us until this century to discover a similar antibiotic. And early-twentieth-century tranquilizers are patterned on a Nigerian witch doctor's success with rauwolfia. There are dozens of such illustrations throughout medical history.

My scholarly journey has taken me to the China of the great Yellow Emperor and his *Classic on Internal Medicine*, to the Egypt of the pharaohs and the Copts, the Greece of Alexander and Aristotle, and the Rome of Julius Caesar. My research has also taken me through India to explore Ayurvedic medicine and Hatha yoga, to the far reaches of the African continent and its traditional healers, and to the land of the Old Testament and its significant hygienic laws. Through many remarkable texts, I have ventured across the deserts of the nomad Bedouins, the million and a half miles of the old Arabian peninsula, and the Japan and Korea influenced by early Chinese medicine. I am indebted also to the Mexican and Native Americans who taught survival medicine to early explorers, hunters, and settlers, the healers of the Caribbean Islands, the medicine men of Hawaii, the early homeopaths, the water healing experts, and always to those unheralded village healers of towns in Algeria, Austria, the Balkans, Belgium, Bohemia, Canada, Denmark, England, Finland, France, Germany, Holland, Hungary, Ireland, Italy, Latvia, Macedonia, Moravia, Morocco, the Netherlands,

Norway, Poland, Rumania, Russia, Scotland, Siberia, Spain, Sweden, and early America.

Much of what we know about the medical practices of antiquity depends on two astonishing first-century historians: Pliny the Elder and Dioscorides. Pliny, a Roman who wrote voluminously on the uses of plants and herbs, left a thirty-seven-volume encyclopedia of the Roman world in which he describes the use of vegetable cures. Dioscorides, a Greek physician, was a surgeon in the Roman army. Modern pharmacology—the science of medicines, poisons, and cures—stems from his attempts to systematize medical knowledge. His book, *De Materia Medica*, was the first known textbook of pharmacology. It became a reference manual used by physicians for the next fifteen hundred years.

Ancient Healing Secrets also includes many remedies using civilization's oldest healing substance—water. I also include the best of the self-help finger pressure therapies, some from the Chinese martial arts, and some from Japanese shiatsu. One source not generally known to the public is the work of Dr. William Fitzgerald, whose easy-to-use finger pressure exercises originated one hundred years ago and are based on the ancient Chinese acupuncture meridians.

For this book, I have studied old family recipes from all parts of the globe, reviewed the work of many botanists, extracted information from ancient texts and famous herbals, and surveyed the journals of explorers and travelers.

I have found the solutions of the past constructive and easy to use. Plant substances mentioned in the book can be obtained either in supermarkets, health food stores or by mail order (see Appendix I).

I wish you good health and constructive delving into the past.

Dian Dincin Buchman, Ph.D.
New York, New York
August, 1995

HOW HERBS WERE PREPARED

Most ancient healers used plant-based medicinals in the form of teas, infusions, decoctions, poultices, or plasters. All were simple to make.

Teas were generally made by dropping an ounce of dried herbs into a pint of boiled, hot water for a minute or two, then straining the liquid and drinking it as needed.

Infusions were made by dropping an ounce of dried herbs into a pint of boiled water, then steeping the herbs for at least fifteen minutes before straining.

Decoctions were made by dropping an ounce of dried herbs into a pint of water while it was boiling—and then leaving it to gently simmer for at least thirty minutes.

Poultices were made from dried or powdered herbs mixed with water, with a healthy scoop of oatmeal or flour to bind it all together. Generally, two ounces of herbs were mixed with about twenty ounces of the binder and enough water to make a paste. The mixture was then placed directly on the skin and covered with a warm cloth or bandage.

Plasters were mixed exactly the same way as a poultice, but because they frequently called for herbs that could irritate the skin, they were folded into a cloth before they were placed on the body.

A GUIDE TO SYMBOLS

PLANT

By far the majority of these ancient remedies are plant-based. Herbs were often the predominant ingredient in tonics, teas and poultices. But ancient healers put every part of all sorts of plants—and even trees—to healing use. Medicines were made from roots, bulbs, bark, leaves, fruit, sap, grains, nuts, flowers, seeds and juice. Many plant foods were also used medicinally.

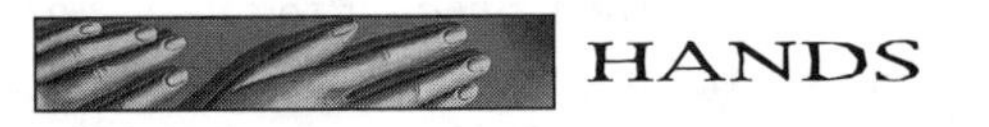

HANDS

The healing power of touch has been recognized for centuries. From ancient Chinese acupressure treatments to simple, time-tested massage techniques, hands-on healing has soothed pain, stimulated immunity and renewed vital energy in cultures all over the world.

WATER

Today, we know about relaxing baths, saunas and hot tubs. In earlier times, water was used for healing in hundreds of inventive ways—as wraps, soaks, steam or ice treatments—to soothe, heal or invigorate. Europeans began to "take the waters" at spas a century ago, and hydrotherapy became an honored healing discipline.

EARTH

Sometimes, the ancients dug deeper than plants for healing remedies—into the earth itself. Earth cures included the use of clay, mud and minerals—often as poultices, or as masks to draw out impurities.

BREATH

Breath is the key to life. And in many traditional healing systems, breathing itself was the source of cure. Healers have long instructed their patients in "conscious breathing" or systematic breathing techniques to relieve various complaints, strengthen lungs, ease pain and soothe stress.

MOVEMENT

Years ago, people used their bodies in everyday life far more than most of us do today. Healing methods of movement—such as T'ai Chi and yoga asanas—and therapeutic exercise have been restoring the human body for hundreds of years. Now as then, a body in motion is a body moving toward better health.

ANIMAL

From enzyme-rich honey to coagulating spiderwebs to medicinal uses of eggs, milk, butter, meat, fish and oils—animals and insects have provided healing foods and remedies to humankind for as long as we've been able to hunt or husband them.

MIND

Many of today's "mind-body medicine" concepts have their roots in the guided meditation, visualization and lucid dreaming secrets of years ago. Whether invoked beside an ancient campfire or from the depths of a favorite armchair, the healing powers of the mind and spirit can prevent or relieve chronic conditions and pain.

ACNE

The Bumpy Horror Show hits girls around age thirteen and boys around sixteen. Just at the moment they want to look their best, the body releases puddles of natural secretions. The face, the back, even the buttocks may break out in unwanted pimples, blackheads, and whiteheads. There are many factors that encourage acne assaults: stress, lack of sleep, hygiene, and sometimes, cosmetics and certain foods. Foods that influence acne attacks in some people are iodine-rich foods such as shellfish, nuts and iodized salt; soft drinks, sharp cheeses, hot coffee, and hot tea.

To keep the skin clear of acne, early pioneer farm women experimented with foods from their own gardens. In farmer Janice Myers' family, wheat water has kept generations of Idaho women clear of acne. DIRECTIONS: Buy wheat berries for sprouting in a health food store or by mail. Soak the wheat berries in pure water for a day. Discard the berries, drink the water. Continue the cleansing drink once a day as long as the acne continues. (See Appendix I for mail-order listings.)

The use of honey for healing is as old as history itself. Egyptians used honey plus wheat or almond oil for healing face masks. Amazingly, when archaeologists opened an Egyptian tomb over three thousand years old, among the discoveries was a woman's cosmetic jar full of perfectly preserved honey. DIRECTIONS: Combine a tablespoon of wheat germ oil with a tablespoon of honey and apply as a mask for fifteen minutes. Wash off with warm water and a soft cloth.

In the past, the women of Barcelona prepared a rosemary and lavender vinegar lotion that they applied to their faces each day to control blemishes. DIRECTIONS: Steep together four ounces of apple cider vinegar, one ounce of lavender flowers, and one ounce of rosemary flowers. Discard the flowers after twenty days. Dilute with eight parts of pure water and use as a cleansing lotion.

Throughout past centuries, the women of Italy, Spain, and France controlled blackheads with herbal steam facials. Many herbs can be used, but one favorite has continued to be the flowers of the chamomile plant. DIRECTIONS: Place a handful of chamomile flowers into a glass, ceramic, or stainless steel bowl. Pour two cups of boiling water over the chamomile. This will generate instant steam. Drape a towel over your head and lean over the bowl, allowing the towel to hang over the bowl and trap the steam. Keep your eyes closed and stay in that position for ten to fifteen minutes. You will feel perspiration dripping, and blackheads will be easier to extract. Wash off the loosened debris with a clean, soft cloth, then pop each blackhead out by squeezing gently with your thumb and index finger. Cover your fingers with a clean tissue. Note that whiteheads, large pimples, or cysts should not be steamed or squeezed.

Catherine the Great was a raw adolescent of fifteen when she arrived at the opulent Russian court from the small duchy of Anhalt-Zerbst. Russian women aristocrats showed her the clay facial masks they used and explained how clay powder can absorb dirt and control excess skin oil. Similar green or white clay and clay masks are available today in better health food stores and pharmacies. DIRECTIONS: It's better to use clay as a full-face mask, not as a spot aid. Purchase from a health food store or pharmacy and follow package directions.

Thousands of years ago the Chinese discovered three trigger points on the face and hands that influence acne outbreaks. DIRECTIONS: Press each point daily. The *Ho Ku* point lies at the edge of the two bones in the webbing between the thumb and the index finger. (Do not stimulate this point if you are pregnant since it may bring on uterine contractions.) The next point is at the inner crease as you bend your arm at the elbow. Bend your arm tightly, place a finger at the end of the crease, and keep your finger in place. The third point is just below the collarbone, in the hollow where your arms join your body.

Every village in Europe has a cabbage remedy to heal infected sores. In Hungary, women add astringents such as lemon and witch hazel to the cabbage. DIRECTIONS: Select a medium cabbage and cut in half. Wash each leaf thoroughly then place in a blender. Squeeze and strain half of a lemon and add to the leaves. Add one cup of distilled witch hazel extract. Blend all three together, then apply twice a day.

ACUTE PAIN

Pain is a bulletin from the body that something is wrong. Acute pain demands immediate treatment. Remedies from long ago include water therapy, pressure therapy, and many first aid treatments using flowers.

In the early 1800s, a doctor named Samuel Hahnemann invented a new approach to health and medicine called "homeopathy." His system relies on using minute doses of what made you sick to heal you—usually in the form of plants and minerals. America is just rediscovering homeopathy, but it has continued to be popular in Europe—the British Royal family relies heavily on it, forty percent of British doctors refer patients to homeopaths, and forty percent of French doctors have studied homeopathy and are able to prescribe it. One of Hahnemann's exceptional first aid discoveries was the use of the alpine flower, arnica, to assuage pain and trauma. DIRECTIONS: In homeopathic first aid, practitioners place tiny Arnica pills under the tongue following any trauma or injury. They feel that this immediately quiets pain. Arnica lotions and ointments are sold as topical treatments for sprains, spasms, pain, and bruises and can be purchased in health food stores, some drug stores, and by mail. They must NOT be used if the skin is abraded or broken. A low dosage such as 6 or 9 (c or x) is useful for first aid.

Centuries ago, cold water was the primary remedy for injuries. Then, in the mid-nineteenth century, an Austrian peasant rediscovered some of the basics of cold water therapy and became a famous local healer. Today, cold water, along with ice, is once again the accepted treatment for sprains, pulls, spasms, and bruises. DIRECTIONS: Apply ice immediately after an injury. Use ice for no more than twenty minutes out of each hour during the first twenty-four hours. After the first day, you can use heat to further reduce stiffness and muscle soreness. Effective heat treatments are application of a hot water bottle, hot showers, or steeping the body in a warm bath. To increase healing, add Epsom, coarse, or sea salt to the bath water. When using showers, accelerate the healing process by alternating from hot to cold water. This stimulates circulation. Always end the session with cool or cold water.

Long ago in antiquity, the Chinese discovered many acupressure points that could be used to combat pain caused by practicing the martial arts of judo and jujitsu. For sudden, darting or shooting pains, apply deep pressure on the *Kroun-Loun* point. This point is located directly over the top of the ankle bone on the outside of the foot. For dull, aching pain, press the *Ro-Kou* point. This point is at the triangle where the bones of the index finger and the thumb meet. Note this is also called the *Ho Ku* point. Do not use this point if you are pregnant.

As far back as the Crusades, the oil-steeped flowers of St. John's Wort (*Hypericum*) were acclaimed for their painkilling and healing abilities. DIRECTIONS: To make St. John's Wort oil, briefly soak a handful of the flowers in two cups of olive oil, then gently heat. Strain out the flowers. Let cool slightly, then apply oil topically. The oil is available from health food stores and mail order. (See Appendix I.)

Rosemary (*Rosmarinus offinallis*), a beloved herb all over the world, is a major ingredient in Hungary Water. Queen Elizabeth of Hungary developed this lotion in the thirteenth century to restore feeling to her paralyzed limbs. The de Medici court in Florence, Italy used still another rosemary lotion for joint and bone pain. DIRECTIONS: To make the lotion, buy an inexpensive bottle of vodka, gin, or brandy. Pour off one-third of the liquid, set it aside, and fill the bottle with rosemary flowers and—if available—rosemary twigs. Steep the bottle in the sun for three days (or keep the bottle near some stove heat). Shake several times a day. Strain and use. Rosemary lotion has a slight sting. Apply gently with a cotton pad. When the skin stops absorbing the liquid, stop patting. Bandage the area with soft flannel. After patting on the liniment, you might also drink rosemary flower tea which is available in health food stores.

Old British herbals describe ways to use aromatic lavender to reduce pain. DIRECTIONS: Enclose fresh or dried lavender flowers in a cloth. Tie with a rubber band. Dip the cloth in very hot water, gently squeeze out, and apply to the area of pain. This heavenly-smelling compress speedily alleviates most recent pains.

For acute facial neuralgia, French village healers often recommended this easy water remedy. DIRECTIONS: Apply hot compresses to the area of pain. Or, if you happen to be in the shower, aim hot shower streams to any areas of facial tension.

For facial pain, use this Asian cheek trigger point. DIRECTIONS: With clean fingers, put the index fingers inside the mouth. Pull and press outward on the cheek, extending it upward toward the ears.

AGE SPOTS

Harmless dark flat spots emerge as we get older. They look like freckles, but they're called "age spots." What causes them? The sun. It triggers the body to produce a substance called melanin, which announces itself as dark spots on the skin. Also there is an increased internal breakdown of materials which eventually shows up as brown spots on the body. There are at least four ways to help prevent this evidence of a long life lived in the sun: Avoid excess sun, use sunscreen, exercise each day, eat a wide variety of fruits and vegetables, and use antioxidant supplements to discourage cellular damage to the skin. The key antioxidants are vitamin C, vitamin E, beta-carotene, and selenium.

Folk medicine from various countries has favored the application of castor oil on age spots. The Palma Christi oil from Heritage Products is a dependable choice. DIRECTIONS: Dab on the oil with a cotton swab. Apply daily as needed.

In the past, many fair-haired German women deliberately ate several raw carrots a day. They believed it helped keep their skin looking young and also helped control age spots. Carrots are one of the many yellow-orange vegetables that contain vast amounts of the antioxidant beta-carotene, a nutrient that may help counteract some of the damage caused by the sun. DIRECTIONS: To control age spots, some nutrition-minded physicians prescribe 50,000 international units (I.U.) of beta-carotene each day. Note that this is considered a high dose, so only take this amount after you've consulted a knowledgeable nutrition expert. And do not take it if you are an alcoholic, or if you have any liver disease.

To lighten brown skin spots, early American settlers in Tennessee mixed fresh lemon juice and buttermilk and gently applied this mask to brown spots. Both buttermilk and lemon are mild skin bleaches that can be used separately. In the past, lemon juice was often combined with rose water and dabbed on the skin to bleach it. Wash off the application and pat oil on the skin to soften it and prevent drying.

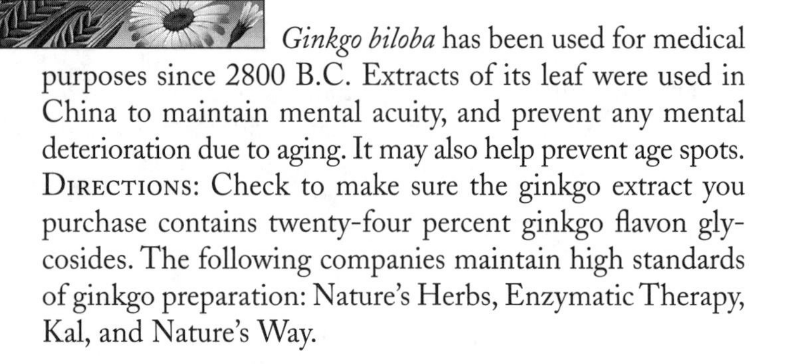

Ginkgo biloba has been used for medical purposes since 2800 B.C. Extracts of its leaf were used in China to maintain mental acuity, and prevent any mental deterioration due to aging. It may also help prevent age spots. DIRECTIONS: Check to make sure the ginkgo extract you purchase contains twenty-four percent ginkgo flavon glycosides. The following companies maintain high standards of ginkgo preparation: Nature's Herbs, Enzymatic Therapy, Kal, and Nature's Way.

Northern Italians are often fair-haired and fair-skinned. Occasionally they use a traditional northern Italian cosmetic poultice to lighten the age spots and freckles that threaten their fair complexions. DIRECTIONS: Beat two whole eggs, add a tablespoon of heavy cream and a teaspoon of Epsom salts, then blend with a fork. Use a cotton swab and apply the mixture to brown spots. Wash off about ten minutes later. To prevent drying the skin, apply oil to the spots afterwards.

Lake Constance is a breathtakingly beautiful area between Switzerland, Germany, and Austria. The local women have a cosmetic tradition to mildly bleach age spots. DIRECTIONS: Grate two tablespoons of horseradish into four tablespoons of milk and simmer for two or three minutes. Gently apply the paste to the age spots. Allow it to dry, then gently wash it off. Apply oil to the area to prevent drying the skin.

Panax ginseng is an ancient Chinese herb mentioned over 2,000 years ago in the Chinese pharmacopoeia, *Shen Nung Pen Ts'ao*. *Panax* means panacea, and this root continues to be used to overcome general problems of aging such as recovery from an illness, low energy levels, impotence, hot flashes, and sensitivity to heat. Chinese, Korean, and Russian studies show ginseng enhances memory and is a general tonic for many of the indispositions of aging. Ginseng is available as a tea, tablet, capsule, powder, and extract.

ANXIETY

"Today is worth two tomorrows" is an axiom of the ancient world where life was short, and it was necessary to deal with problems quickly. Our forebears had many strategies for dealing with anxiety, including the following age-old healing secret: Asking one's dreams for the solution to anxiety-producing problems.

Ancient Greek priest-physicians practiced their art in huge temples of health called *Asclepieia*. Patients were encouraged to sleep in these vast sanatoriums, and their dreams were interpreted to create cures. DIRECTIONS: Today you can duplicate this technique for even minor anxiety problems. Before sleep, prepare your bedroom so that there is some fresh air coming in. Place a pad and pencil by your bedside. Take a long, warm, relaxing bath. Get into bed. Take the pad in your hand and start thinking, "What is my major problem?" Concisely summarize one problem. Then in three sentences or less, address your-soon-to-be-sleeping-mind and write: "Dreams, how can I....?" You might write, for example: "Dreams, how can I get to work on time?" or "Dreams, how can I get my boss to like me more?" or "Dreams, how can I get Johnny to do better in school?" or "Dreams, how can I eat less?" Address only one problem per night! After writing down the question, go to sleep. The dreaming mind, once instructed, acts like a new-age computer, analyzing and solving problems. In three days or less, you'll have one or several answers just pop into your brain, and you'll have one less problem to cause you anxiety.

Chamomile has been used for centuries by Europeans as a calming and relaxing table tea. DIRECTIONS: Have a cup whenever you're feeling anxious. Use one tablespoon of dried flowers for each cup of boiling water. Steep and strain. Any leftover tea can be added to your bath to boost the natural relaxing effect of warm water.

Valerian root is a favorite European herb used to calm anxiety. Its popularity throughout Imperial Russia and other parts of Europe was so entrenched over the centuries that it is mentioned in many old plays and novels —including those of Chekhov and Tolstoy. DIRECTIONS: Since this root has an unattractive aroma, it is better to purchase valerian tincture or pills in a health food store or by mail. When using a liquid tincture, add eight to sixteen drops to a favorite herbal tea or calming bath.

In old-time melodrama, the distressed heroine is always wringing her hands. It turns out this an instinctive and helpful motion. Massaging, pulling, pressing, and tapping the hands inhibits the transmission of nerve impulses through the body and lessens reactions to stress. For centuries Chinese martial arts experts have used finger pressure on two specific hand points to release tension. DIRECTIONS: The *Tchong-Tchrong* point is on the topside of the hand, at the bottom of the middle nail, on the side nearest the index finger. The *Chenn-Menn* point to free up anxiety is on the palm side, just above the wrist under the line of the fourth finger. Another key place for overcoming anxiety is on the sole of the foot under the fleshy part of the metatarsal, under the middle toe. Gently rub or press on any of these points whenever you feel tense.

Over time, the French have developed an affinity for lime flower tea to ease anxiety, depression, and hysteria. The lime tree is also known as the linden tree. Prolonged baths in infusions of the flowers are helpful, particularly to calm panic attacks. DIRECTIONS: Take several handfuls of the flowers, add to a quart of water, and simmer for fifteen minutes. Steep until there is a rich color. Strain out the flowers, then add the tea to a warm bath.

Just as quick, nervous breathing reenforces anxiety, the taking of long, deep breaths instantly reduces anxiety. Indian Yogis have found that rhythmic breathing cuts down on stress. DIRECTIONS: One easy yoga breathing routine is the six-three-six method of quick relaxation. Inhale through your nose to the count of six. Gently hold your breath for a count of three. Next exhale for a count of six. In for six, hold for three, exhale for six. Repeat several times.

In 1814, a pharmacist published *A New and Complete American Medical Family Herbal*, a book which includes an exceptional antiseptic tonic of sage, cinnamon, ginger, angelica root, and cloves steeped in Madeira wine. The amounts used here are adjusted for modern kitchens. DIRECTIONS: Make a strong sage tea with a handful of sage and a pint of boiled water. Steep and strain. Add a pinch of powdered cinnamon, a pinch of powdered ginger, a pinch of dried cloves, and a small piece of angelica root. Pour the herbs into a bottle of Madeira or port wine. Steep for an hour. Strain the wine through a fine mesh strainer or muslin. Put it in well-corked bottles and store it in a cool cellar or refrigerator. "Use in all debility, lowness of spirits, and dejection of mind." Take half a wine glass every morning and before dinner.

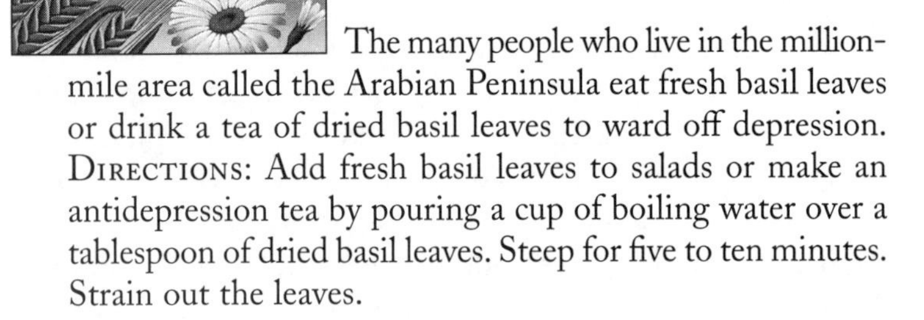

The many people who live in the million-mile area called the Arabian Peninsula eat fresh basil leaves or drink a tea of dried basil leaves to ward off depression. DIRECTIONS: Add fresh basil leaves to salads or make an antidepression tea by pouring a cup of boiling water over a tablespoon of dried basil leaves. Steep for five to ten minutes. Strain out the leaves.

ARTHRITIS

Anthropologists have discovered that even the most primitive people suffered from some sort of joint inflammation or wear and tear. In the past, old herbals, family receipt books, and local healers all concerned themselves with potions and remedies for a disease they called "rheumatism"—or what we call osteoarthritis. Everyone seemed to have a touch of it!

The famous first-century Greek doctor Dioscorides traveled widely with the Roman army and was a careful observer of the medicine of his time. In his writings, he describes the use of a substance he calls "oxymel," or sour honey, for arthritis-like pains. Over the centuries, oxymel—a combination of apple cider vinegar and honey—has been widely used to dissolve painful calcium deposits in the body and for other health problems, such as hayfever. DIRECTIONS: Oxymel is simple to make. Combine equal amounts of apple cider vinegar and a pure honey. Use a teaspoon or a tablespoon to one cup or glass of pure water. Add eight times the amount of water to the oxymel. It will taste like apple juice. Oxymel can also be sipped throughout the day to calm nervous adults and restless children.

Drinking potato juice water on an empty stomach each morning is a beloved century-old European arthritis remedy. DIRECTIONS: Peel an organically grown potato and drop it in the blender with a six- or eight-ounce glass of pure water. Drink the juice. To prepare the remedy without using a blender, cut a potato in slices and soak it in a glass of water overnight. Strain and drink the juice.

Strong spikes of arthritic pain during a long Siberian winter frequently called for bran and onion. DIRECTIONS: Right after dinner, take a handful of bran and one large white onion broken into individual "leaves." Place the bran in a quart of water and bring to a boil. Simmer for ten minutes or so. Deposit the bran water in a pan large enough to immerse the hurtful joint or joints. Soak the joint for fifteen minutes. Dry the area. Next, loosely apply layer upon layer of raw onion leaves on the joint or joints. Cover with a plastic bag and attach with a loose Ace bandage. Leave on for several hours. Before going to bed, unwind the Ace bandage, lift the onion leaves, and gently wash the skin. Do not dry. Rebind the onion bandage until morning. Repeat on consecutive nights as needed.

For arthritis and other such conditions, old European wisdom recommends the increase of sweating in order to discharge "toxins" from the body. DIRECTIONS: Once a week, add a teaspoon of hayflower extract or a cupful of Epsom salts to a steaming, hot bath. Then get right into bed after the bath, cover up, and sweat it out. Note these baths have a powerful detoxifying action. Do not use this remedy if you are pregnant or if you have high blood pressure or heart trouble.

Another European approach to arthritis is a cold water friction massage to give the circulation to joints a boost. DIRECTIONS: Cover the body with a towel to avoid a draft and only expose one area at a time. Dip a washcloth or a massage mitt in cold water, wring it out, and rub the bare area. Dry and cover. Move from one section of the body to the next until the entire body is invigorated and refreshed.

Many island cultures discovered that eating fresh pineapple greatly affects arthritis. Bromelain, the enzyme in pineapple, lessens the pain of swelling in soft tissues. DIRECTIONS: Each day, eat several pieces of fresh pineapple or take four to six tablets of bromelain. The tablets are available in health food stores.

German settlers brought a mainstay in European folk medicine to America—the concept of a healing castor oil compress. DIRECTIONS: Heat about two tablespoons of castor oil in a nonaluminum pot. Soak a small, clean (flannel, if available) cloth in the oil. Apply the soaked compress to the aching joint, being careful not to burn yourself. To keep the heat in and protect your clothes, cover the compress with plastic and cover the plastic with a larger towel. Keep the compress on for thirty minutes. Repeat the application as often as necessary, but only when the joint is not inflamed. Deodorized castor oil is available in health food stores and through the mail. (See Appendix I.)

Hungarian and other European peasants traditionally used white cabbage leaf poultices to relieve arthritis pain. DIRECTIONS: To use cabbage, discard top ribbed leaves. Mince about five inside leaves into small pieces and place into a bowl. Add several tablespoons of chamomile or lavender tea water. Roll the mixture in a soft cotton cloth and apply the cabbage poultice to the painful area.

For centuries, Europeans brewed beer and ale with hops, a practice which was thought to improve both sleep and appetite. Since it was also generally believed that hops could extract calcium deposits from the body, hops beer became a favorite arthritis remedy. In rural England, folks drank many nonintoxicating beers made with hops and a variety of herbs such as cleansing nettle or dandelion. Dandelion stout was a favored home brew. DIRECTIONS: To make a hops tea, steep two tablespoons of hop flowers in a cup of boiled water for ten minutes. Strain out the flowers. Drink the tea in the early part of the day only.

In an acute attack of arthritis, it is an old established custom for French villagers to apply a buttercup poultice. DIRECTIONS: Place six handfuls of buttercup leaves and flowers in a quart of water. Bring to a mild boil, remove from heat, and steep. Strain out the buttercup mash, roll it in a soft cloth, and apply.

In the remote mountains of Tennessee, folks still use poke roots to allay pain. While poke roots are not safe internally, a long time ago these hardy mountain people discovered they could use charred, powdered roots as a topical application. Note the placement of the remedy—on the feet. "It will draw pain out anywhere in the body," say present-day mountaineers. DIRECTIONS: Roast a few poke roots in a fire. Scrape and clean charred sections with a knife. Grind the remaining root into a powder. Place the powder in a thin cloth or apply directly to the bottom of the feet.

ASTHMA

Asthma is a potentially life-threatening condition marked by repeated attacks of coughing and wheezing due to spasms of the bronchi in the lungs. Some cases of asthma are a reaction to allergens. If attacks occur mainly after an asthma victim lies down, modern physicians suspect acid reflux: see Heartburn. Historically, local healers have used a variety of methods to ease the condition.

Past German herbalists learned an indirect method that could control asthma attacks. DIRECTIONS: First, frightened patients were instructed to breathe in and out in a slow, deliberate manner. Next, healers strove to divert blood from the heart by bathing the arms of the patient and applying a cloth briefly dipped into hot lemon balm tea or hot hayflower extract over the heart area.

To lessen asthma spasms, last century's Father Kunzle, a German Swiss master herbalist, recommended an arm bath in which he applied a hot cider "wash." DIRECTIONS: Heat several cups of very old fermented cider or apple cider vinegar to a boil. Take it off the heat and soak several dish towels in the liquid. When you can touch the towels, wring them out and apply, as hot as possible, to the arms.

The exquisite port city of Amalfi, Italy, is known as "lemon land." The delightful aroma of lemon is everywhere and the inhabitants have a long tradition of using lemons and limes as an asthma remedy. DIRECTIONS: Drink lemon juice diluted with cold water every morning as soon as you wake up. Between meals, drink one teaspoon of undiluted lime juice.

In Japanese *shiatsu,* practitioners massage several points of the upper back to ease asthma. DIRECTIONS: Asthma patients should have other people massage their entire back area. Two easily-reached trigger point areas for asthma control are the sides of the nostrils, and the chest. Tap gently on all these areas as needed.

The early Roman historian Pliny wrote that the ancient Egyptians used raw garlic and garlic juice to heal asthma-like coughs. DIRECTIONS: Add several cloves of garlic to the juice of processed carrots and beets and drink. Or add the clove to six ounces of V-8 juice and drink. Either way, it's a healing and cleansing drink.

Fast breathing and unending coughing are exhausting for the asthma victim. In India and China, ancient doctors taught patients to breathe in a slow sustained way. DIRECTIONS: First slow down by mentally counting backwards from ten to one. Draw in a deep, long breath and exhale as slowly as possible. Continue to breathe in this controlled fashion, and agitation will disappear.

In the great oral tradition of village healing, Russians from the Crimea describe this traditional breathing and water-sipping remedy to halt an asthma attack. DIRECTIONS: The patient is told to breathe in and out very slowly and to be aware of the need to breathe deliberately. In between breaths, the patient is asked to sip two glasses of tepid water. The entire exercise should take about thirty minutes.

ATHLETE'S FOOT

Athlete's foot is an annoying, irritating fungal skin infection. It frequently begins between the third and fourth toes, and later can invade other toes, toenails, and the skin over the arch. Infected toenails become thickened and distorted. The pain, inflammation, and itching can range from slight to severe.

The island people of Jamaica have always controlled athlete's foot infections with a garlic massage. DIRECTIONS: Wash the affected foot in soapy water. Rinse and dry well. Peel fresh garlic and massage onto the area of infection twice a day, until the foot looks clear and healthy. To prevent recurrences, Jamaicans follow up with a twice-a-week garlic massage.

Russian peasants also used garlic as a fungus remedy. DIRECTIONS: The curative lotion combines eight ounces of peeled, minced garlic with four ounces of olive oil. Keep the mixture in a warm place for three days. Strain out the garlic and apply the oil to a well-cleaned, rinsed, and dried foot area. Use once or twice a week as a preventive measure. Often peasants added small amounts of anise, caraway, or cinnamon oil to mask the garlic odor.

Captain James Cook was sent to Tahiti by the British in 1768 on a secret mission. On this voyage, he discovered the island of New Zealand, then went west to Australia. One of his many discoveries was the way the aborigines used leaves of the tea tree for first aid. Nothing much was done with this herbal find until the First World War when Australian soldiers used the leaves of the tea tree to guard against insect bites and skin infections. Current research on the tea tree shows the oil from the leaves is an excellent *external* antibacterial, antifungicidal remedy. DIRECTIONS: For external fungal infections, apply tea tree oil with a disposable cotton swab every day. This oil is available in local health food stores and by mail order. (See Appendix I.)

Over the past centuries, Chinese doctors controlled the problem of damp and itchy toes by firmly applying pressure to the upper part of the foot.

Directions: Press deeply on the foot at the separation point between the fourth and smallest toes. Wash hands afterwards and dry them with a disposable paper towel.

American pioneers used the residue of cooked and fermented apples—apple cider vinegar—as their athlete's foot remedy. Directions: Soak a cloth in apple cider vinegar, wring out, and apply overnight to foot. Repeat as often as necessary.

BACK PAIN

There have been backaches ever since the first human bent down to pick something up. In fact, backaches may be one of the most frequent problems in the world. In the old days, backaches were called "lumbago," and old medical books and oral tradition are flooded with backache solutions. Actually, there are a lot of natural approaches that can subdue this problem, including plant ointments, massage, finger pressure, and stretches which release pressure on the spine, and safe, old-fashioned posture alignment secrets. Ohashi, a modern Japanese *shiatsu* teacher, advises tired people to avoid backaches by resting frequently. "Lie on your side and bend your body so it is shaped like a shrimp," says Ohashi. This sage advice from the past matches the present-day instructions of orthopedists who remind backache patients to sleep in a fetal position with a pillow under their knees.

The British have always put a great store on proper posture, and a long time ago they devised this simple exercise to decrease back tension and ease a minor ache. Directions: As often as you can during the day, stand against a wall, heels touching the wall with feet six inches apart. Then do this checklist: Are my hips touching the wall? Are my shoulders touching the wall? Is my head touching the wall? If the answer is "yes" to all questions, move away from the wall but retain that same erect posture. Hold on to this sensation of erectness as long as possible.

Late in the last century, Bavarian Sebastian Kneipp helped to categorize the many benefits of water therapy. For back spasm, he taught patients to apply an extremely cold cloth or to ice the area of pain. After the first acute stage, it is useful to try moist heat such as a hot water bottle or hot cloth compress to relax the back. DIRECTIONS: Soak a cloth in ice water or wrap the cloth around a handful of ice. Lie down and ask a friend to place the cloth on your back. Leave in place for fifteen to twenty minutes. Do this several times during the first twenty-four hours your back hurts. Then switch to warm compresses and hot water bottles.

In the last century, hardy Swedes who immigrated to Minnesota discovered that pouring buckets of hot water on the back could often prevent backaches from developing. DIRECTIONS: To take a preventive Swedish shower today, stand with knees slightly bent and both hands on your thighs just above the knee. Rest as much weight as you can on your arms in order to relieve the pressure on your back. Allow the water to play on your back for about ten minutes.

Deep breathing is a strong factor in controlling backache. To keep the back strong, Chinese of all ages perform *t'ai chi,* an ancient breathing and weight-bearing exercise. In fact, people in factories throughout Asia often do special breathing exercises. Every hour a bell rings for a breathing, stretching, and yawning break! Singapore healers teach a particular stretch to prevent chronic backaches. DIRECTIONS: Standing or sitting take a deep breath, raise your arms to shoulder height, and stretch your fingers until you can feel a pull on the fourth and fifth fingers. This will make you feel as if you're floating upwards. Repeat often during the day.

BOILS

A boil is a hard, painful skin eruption that contains a core of pus. It's caused by a staphylococcus germ which enters through a hair follicle. The first defense against boils is immaculate cleanliness, which is why many early cultures developed elaborate bath rituals. The Israelis, the Japanese, and the Romans were early leaders in hygiene in the ancient world. Much later the Scandinavians, the Germans, and the Russians established bath, steam, and sauna therapy for cleanliness and general health.

Hungarian village healers traditionally applied dried grapes in order to cure boils. DIRECTIONS: Buy unseeded natural and unsulphured raisins and crush about a dozen into a paste. Bandage the raisin paste over the boil for about half a day. Discard this paste and apply another one that's freshly made. The boil should disappear. If it doesn't, see your doctor.

Early in the last century, German healers discovered two ways to control boils. One was an ice application to abort the boil before it emerged; the other was a series of hot applications when and if the boil surfaced. DIRECTIONS: At the first sign of redness or skin puckering, immediately rub the potential boil area with ice.

If the ice is not used quickly enough and a boil emerges, apply wet heat as a weapon. Use hot, wet cloths over the area to open up the blood vessels and make the infection come to a head. DIRECTIONS: Fold a small hand towel and dip it into extremely hot water. Wring it out and apply it to the boil. Cover the hot, wet towel with a dry towel. Keep on for twenty minutes. Repeat many times. To avoid later contamination, make sure to wash and *boil* these towels or use clean disposable cloths.

Swiss herbalists always believed in addressing the internal cause of boils. Patients who had the misfortune of frequent boil attacks were advised to go on a water and vegetable-juice fast. DIRECTIONS: Sip pure water mixed with beet and carrot juice in small amounts all through the day for at least three days, but no more than seven. This will help to purify the body. Check with your doctor first if you have any pre-existing medical problems.

Jeannette Ysaye, widow of Belgian violinist and conductor Eugene Ysaye, believed that fresh cottage cheese has an amazing ability to draw out heat and infection and will even soften hard swellings. DIRECTIONS: Mash fresh cottage cheese and apply directly to the hardened area of the skin.

Native Americans taught early explorers and settlers how to treat and cure infections with peach twigs, leaves, and peach pit tea. DIRECTIONS: For the tea, combine two cups of water with two clean peach pits and boil for twenty minutes. Take out the pits and reserve. Soak a cloth or a cotton pad in the hot tea, squeeze out the water, and apply the hot peach-tea compress to the boil. Repeat.

The boil usually comes to a head in half a day. To make sure you always have a supply of pits on hand, clean, reserve, and freeze pits at the height of the growing season. They may be used several times before you discard them.

To open and clear a boil, Slavic Europeans used a poultice of egg, sugar, lard, and flour. Siberians didn't use flour, but instead insisted on using well-chewed rye bread which, they say, has special curative factors. A chewed bread poultice is an old tradition in Russia. Sometimes Russians combined the chewed bread with two other curative foods: honey and minced onions. It is interesting to note the use of chewed bread, particularly since an American medical researcher looking for new antibiotics discovered that the human tongue contains and emits its own protective antibiotic. DIRECTIONS: One egg yolk, one tablespoon of mashed white sugar, one tablespoon of vegetable lard or butter, and one tablespoon of wheat flour (or chewed rye bread). Grind the ingredients together into a salve and bandage on the hardened area. Apply three times a day for three days. When the boil breaks open, wash the area with boiled water, and keep on applying the mixture.

High in the Smoky Mountains, there are Americans who emigrated from Britain in the eighteenth century. Because they live in an isolated area, they have kept the speech, manners, and home remedies of Britain. They have several remedies for boils, but often prefer to use raw potato. "This will draw the risin' (boil) to a head," says one old-timer. DIRECTIONS: Peel the skin off an uncooked white potato and discard. Then peel white shavings until you have a pile. Apply the shavings to the boil with a clean cloth. Bind the cloth with gauze tape or an elastic bandage.

BONE REGENERATION

A young man was in a motorcycle accident in rural India. To his surprise, he was taken to the home of an Indian "bone-setter," a member of a sect who specialized in setting bones. The man quickly applied a several-thousand-year-old secret plant remedy to set the man's fracture. He did a flawless job, and the bone healed. How? Well, bone cells are in a constant state of flux. The cells live and die and are constantly replaced—in fact, healthy adults replace their entire skeleton every eight years. And all through history, healers have believed that there were ways to encourage this process. By all means, however, if you have sustained a fracture, get yourself to the emergency room!

The warrior Scots always believed in the power of oatmeal and oat groats to build and regenerate bones and ligaments. DIRECTIONS: Eat oatmeal or drink oat tea for breakfast. Make oat tea with one tablespoon of steel-cut oats and one cup of boiling water. Steep, strain, then drink the tea left behind.

Legends of the power of Boneset (*Eupatorium perfoliatum*) come down from an ancient oral tradition. Eupator, king of Pontus, from whom the plant received its name, praised the plant for its medicinal values. The plant has become famous over the centuries for healing aching bones and helping to set broken ones. DIRECTIONS: Apply the flowers and/or leaves as a wet poultice to the area to be healed. Then add a cup of boiled water to one tablespoon of flowers or leaves for tea. The taste is exceptionally bitter. Drink one half cup in the morning; another at night.

Many southwestern Indian tribes used common dandelion for both food and medicine. Fresh young leaves are edible before the plant has flowered, and the roots will make a weak, nonacidic coffee. The Tewas tribe treated fractures by grinding fresh dandelion leaves, adding water, and making a paste. The wet paste was applied to broken bones.

Century upon century ago, gifted Chinese doctors found that specific skin pressure could stimulate bone-cell regeneration and encourage bones to knit. DIRECTIONS: Press on either side of the spine—about one thumb-width away from the spine—right at shoulder level. To stimulate bone cells, Chinese monks practicing *Dao Yin* yoga also recommended daily, rhythmic drumming of the heels on the ground.

Old Kentucky mountain people lived far away from doctors. To set a broken arm, they made a mixture of red clay and water, set splints on each side of the arm, and plastered the splints with the local red clay. When the clay dried, they put the arm in a sling.

Ancient medicine is still practiced in the vast area of the Arabian Peninsula. In this area, there are special bone setters who use a variety of herbal plasters, including a popular one made of lentils and egg white. More complex fractures are set with various resins such as myrrh and egg white. During recovery, a special diet of honey from dates is prescribed.

BRUISES

A bruise is an injury in which blood collects under the skin. The area turns black and blue, and the bruise can swell and cause pain. Those who bruise easily may have a need for extra vitamin C in their diet.

From time immemorial, water has been the first remedy for bruises. Directions: Wash a simple abrasion in warm water and soap, then apply ice wrapped in a cloth. Ice stops the internal bleeding and reduces inflammation. Apply ice ten to twenty minutes of every hour for the first twenty-four hours after an injury. NEVER use heat in the first twenty-four hours.

Many homeopaths have used the yellow-flowered arnica since the early 1800s to control trauma and pain in the body. Directions: Immediately after an injury, ingest four homeopathic Arnica pills under the tongue (usually the 6 or 9 x or c dose). This is usually repeated every fifteen minutes or on the hour during an acute stage of pain. Also apply Arnica lotion or ointment topically *if* the skin is unbroken. Homeopathic Arnica pills and ointments are available in health food stores or by mail. (See Appendix I.)

Old British herbals advise grinding caraway seed and applying the paste directly or in a cloth to a bruise, noting that it "taketh away blacke and blew spots of blows and bruises."

Chinese martial arts experts discovered there were important points to press when bruises needed healing. Directions: If the bruised skin is abraded and broken, press the *Iang-Koann* point on the spine. It's at the point of the fifth lumbar, just above the buttocks. If the skin is not broken, press the *Tsienn-Iu* point at the very tip of each shoulder.

Every European peasant once knew the healing worth of apple cider vinegar for bruises on unbroken skin. Directions: To accelerate healing, dip a cloth into the vinegar and apply directly to the bruise.

The British botanist John Gerard compiled his famous *Herball* in 1597. He observed the value of marjoram in lessening the black and blue marks that appear as a bruise is healing. Directions: To accelerate healing and control black and blue marks, Gerard recommended combining a teaspoon of marjoram tea with a tablespoon of honey and smearing it on bruises.

The lowly onion was a well-known American pioneer first-aid secret for bumps and bruises. Directions: Slice an onion and place it on the bruise to immediately reduce swelling and pain.

BURNS

Minor burns can easily be treated at home with a number of old-fashioned water, food, and plant remedies. First-degree burns cause redness, pain, and mild swelling. Second-degree burns extend below the skin and are characterized by blisters as well as redness, pain, and swelling. Third-degree burns show tissue damage. All burns require the immediate application of ice or cold water. Third degree burns require medical help.

In ancient societies, people usually applied cold water to heal minor burns. The value of this treatment was rediscovered during World War ll when burning seamen jumped into the sea during bombing raids and survived their burns. Today, doctors advise immediate applications of ice water for minor burns. Directions: Immerse injured part into ice water or apply clean, "icy" cloths to the burn. Use the water or cloth for as long as tolerable. (Sometimes the intense cold goes to the head. If this happens stop the treatment for a few moments, and continue as soon as possible.) Repeat these short applications several times during each hour. The ice water will often turn charred black blisters to clean, white flat blisters. Do not place ice itself directly on the skin. It may damage cells by freezing them.

The aloe plant originally came from East and South Africa. It's cultivated in tropical countries, but it also flourishes in countries bordering the Mediterranean. For centuries, the country wisdom in Valencia, Spain, was to apply aloe gel after first dousing a burn with cold water. Most of us can keep a small aloe plant as part of our windowsill medical arsenal. It's a perfect aid for burn emergencies. DIRECTIONS: Break off a leaf, slit it open, and dribble the aloe juice on the burn. Aloe juice heals the skin and prevents scarring.

There are many very reliable sunburn remedies from the remote past. DIRECTIONS: For severe sunburn, many Europeans took healing baths after adding two or more cups of apple cider vinegar to the bath water. Cornstarch baths were also used to heal sunburned skin. DIRECTIONS: Add one half to a pound of cornstarch to a tub of water for a healing bath.

During the centuries when the first pyramids were being built, Egyptians used and praised barley as a remedy for minor burns. DIRECTIONS: Mash together a handful of cooked barley, a handful of unsliced bread without the crust, and a small amount of cooking oil. Bandage the paste onto the burn.

Perhaps we should not be surprised that raw potatoes were a favorite burn remedy of the people of Ireland. DIRECTIONS: Peel, shred, or mince an uncooked white potato and place the pieces of potato on the burn. In thirty minutes or so, the redness of the burn disappears. Sometimes the potato even prevents blistering.

Use the *Chou-Kou* jujitsu point to relieve the pain of burns and scalds. DIRECTIONS: Apply finger pressure as needed on the outside of the foot, about one inch from the end of the little toe.

The coastline of Norway is characterized by numerous islands and breathtaking fjords. In the past, when village Norwegians were confronted with minor burns, they treated them with milk. DIRECTIONS: Soak a cloth in milk and apply the cloth to the burn.

CAVITIES

Just what did people do to clean their teeth before the toothbrush was invented? They used twigs from special trees. Many such twigs are still in use in Africa and Asia. In India, storytellers recount the legend of the Hindu prince, Siddhartha, who lived five hundred years before Christ was born. He became famed in India for his holiness, and he was named the Buddha, "The Enlightened One." It is said that one of the Buddha's discarded toothbrush-twigs grew into an enormous tree. In some parts of India and Pakistan, they still use the same type of twig to whiten and cleanse teeth. In fact, twigs and powder from the Peelu tree are sold in some health food stores and through the mail. (See Appendix I.)

Inhabitants of Bologna, Italy, still use this old sage-leaf remedy for temporary relief of a toothache. DIRECTIONS: In a teapot, pour a cup of boiling water over two tablespoons of fresh or dried sage leaves. Steep and strain. Sip and swish the hot sage tea inside your mouth near the aching tooth. Repeat every fifteen minutes or so. Reserve some of the tea and soak a clean, folded cloth in the hot liquid. Wring out the cloth and apply it to the cheek over the aching area.

Hawaiian healers invented this ginger-root toothache remedy. DIRECTIONS: Roast or cook a small piece of ginger. Shape the ginger to fit over the troubled tooth. Bite down on the ginger for as long as possible. Let the saliva flow through the mouth and "marinate" the tooth. Relief often follows immediately. Repeat the procedure if necessary.

The British, French, and Germans have used homeopathic principles and products since the early 1800s. Arnica is excellent for injuries and trauma and, within the last fifty years or so, has been used by dental patients before, during, and after difficult dental procedures. DIRECTIONS: One half hour to one hour before any severe dental work, place four 6x or 6c, or 9x or 9c of the tiny Arnica pills under the tongue. You can buy Arnica pills from health food stores or mail order companies selling homeopathic remedies. (See Appendix I.)

Chinese first aid includes these martial art points to control pain before, during, and after severe dental work. Directions (before dental work): Press on the *Chenn-*

Menn point on the crease of the inner (palm side) wrist, in line with the little finger. Also press the *Tchong-Tchrong* point under the nail of the middle finger, on the side toward the thumb. DIRECTIONS (DURING DENTAL WORK): Press the *Chang-Iang* point just behind the corner of the fingernail of the index finger, on the side closest to the thumb, as needed. DIRECTIONS (AFTER DENTAL WORK): Press the *Iang-Koann* point on the spine at the fifth lumbar vertebra every two hours. To find the right spot, imagine a line drawn between the midforearms. The spot where it crosses the spine is where you should press.

Witch hazel has been used for bleeding since the pioneers learned about it from Native Americans. DIRECTIONS: After extractions, bite down on cotton pads soaked in witch hazel to reduce swelling and control the bleeding.

The clove tree originates in Indonesia but now grows in other areas of Africa and the Indian Ocean. Many African tribes such as the Bemba and the Zulu use the tree's nail-shaped dried flower buds (*Szygium aromaticum*) as a remedy for toothache. The hard buds are quick to release a volatile oil when scratched by a fingernail. The oil of cloves, Eugenol, is still widely used throughout the world in dentistry to deaden the pain of toothache and check tooth decay. Current investigators have also discovered that clove extract inhibits dental plaque, one cause of cavities.

CHILLS

During cold weather, rain can chill us "to the bone." But many people with circulation problems get chills even in moderate temperatures. Ancient medicine offers remedies for chills no matter what the cause.

Warming the hands can sometimes be as simple as rubbing them together to create some friction. Ancient Asians also discovered that shallow stimulation of the palms, fingers, and upper part of the hand could promote warmth and overcome chills. Directions: Gently scratch the teeth of a comb from wrist to finger tips first on the back of your hand, then on your palm.

In northern Europe, where the weather easily turns from somewhat brisk to deep chill, great store was placed in three water remedies to offset the crisp bite of the cold: hot foot baths, hot baths, and communal steam baths. In Finland and other Scandinavian countries, dry heat saunas and steam baths are ended either by jumping in the snow or by plunging into cold water pools. This stimulates an extraordinary feeling of rejuvenation and exhilaration. Directions: To immediately warm the feet, run a few inches of hot water for a foot bath and add one to two tablespoons of mustard powder. Place feet in the shallow bath for up to ten minutes. For a total body-warming bath, fill the tub with hot water and add a few drops of peppermint essence, a cup of peppermint tea, or several tablespoons of pine essence.

The old martial arts points to raise body temperature are on the shoulder near the neck. Directions: Press deeply on the *Tienn-Tsiao* point on the shoulder, about one thumb-length from the edge of the neck.

In extra-cold Siberia, people improved their circulation and reaction to the extreme cold by following old traditions. Directions: Avoid rapid changes of temperature from one extreme to another. Once or twice a week, take a hot Epsom salt bath just before bedtime. (Do not take hot baths if you have heart trouble, high blood pressure, or are pregnant.) Once a week, vigorously rub your body with a rough cloth. And once in a while, sit briefly in a cold, shallow sitz bath. The friction rub and the sitz bath help institute vigorous circulation patterns.

Notes from the settlers who tamed the West include a curious instruction to put the wooly leaves of mullein in stockings. This was used to keep the feet warm. The leaves of mullein have a whitish, soft dense mass of hairs on both sides, making them feel thick to the touch. Directions: Since mullein hairs might be slightly irritating on naked feet, anyone who tries this today should probably put the leaves in their shoes rather than in their socks or stockings.

During the last century, Spanish village doctors employed indirect water therapy for people with impaired circulation. Directions: Patients were always told never put heat directly on the hands or feet. Instead, patients were to apply hot towels to the torso, an area that shares nerves and blood vessels with the hands and feet.

COLDS

Do you remember this rule of three for colds? "It takes three days to get a cold, three days to have a cold, and three days to get over a cold." This adage reminds us that body signals can be alarm bells—in this case that a cold is brewing. If you are sensitive to your body's signals, you can frequently stop a cold—which is caused by a virus—before it emerges. Antibiotics have no effect on viruses, so old remedies and approaches are practical and useful.

All over the world, from remote time until the present, ginger root has been used as a cold remedy.

Ginger is a revitalizing herb, and raw, peeled slices, or powdered ginger in hot tea, hot soup, or food will reenergize the body. DIRECTIONS: A half cup of ginger tea in your bathwater increases perspiration, which some people feel helps to shorten the cold. Ginger tonic wine is also a great cold antagonist. Well in advance of the typical cold season, buy an inexpensive white or red table wine. Pour off an ounce or two. Wash and cut about a two-inch piece of ginger root into the wine. Recork the bottle. Place the bottle in a dark place for a week to ten days. Strain out the ginger. Label it "Ginger Tonic Wine." At the first sign of a cold, add two tablespoons of the ginger wine to any hot herbal tea such as fennel, peppermint, or vervain before going to sleep. Do not use wines if you are sulphide sensitive, but instead, add boiling water to slices of ginger for a ginger tea.

During the latter part of the last century, Dr. William. H. Fitzgerald studied advanced ear, nose, and throat medicine at a major hospital in Austria. There he was exposed to Chinese acupuncture concepts. Using Chinese meridians—ancient channels of energy found throughout the body—he soon devised his own sector therapy. As a specialist, he must have been astonished to discover that mere pressure on the thumbs could control nasal secretion! To stop a runny nose with the Fitzgerald system, apply *strong* finger pressure to the top and bottom joints of each thumb. After much experimentation, Fitzgerald also realized he could use fat rubberbands to increase the pressure on the joints. DIRECTIONS: Wind a wide band around one thumb joint at a time. Leave it on for no more than fifteen minutes. Take off the rubber band if it hurts or if the area becomes purplish. Repeat, again and again until the nose stops dripping fluids.

Methods of aborting colds utilizing body trigger points show up all over the world. Early settlers from the Scandinavian countries brought with them old country customs which have been passed on through generations of families. Wisconsinite Arny Neilsen remembers his great-grandfather's adage: "At the first sign of a cold coming on, ice the two big toes." Mr. Neilsen says the icing seems to help.

The Chinese use a certain foot point to influence colds and flu. DIRECTIONS: Deeply press the sole of the foot under the fleshy part of the metatarsal that leads to the middle toe.

Ukrainian villagers used mustard paste on the heel of the foot to abort a runny nose. Mustard powder is one of the best remedies in herbal medicine. It quickly brings blood to the surface of the skin, and this starts a healing process. DIRECTIONS: To protect against the "heat" mustard evokes, lightly oil the heels of each foot. Combine one tablespoon of powdered mustard—available in the condiment section of your supermarket—with three tablespoons of flour and half a tablespoon of tepid water. The paste should not be loose or runny. The Ukrainians apply it directly to the heels of the foot, although you can use it encased in cloth as a poultice. After applying the mustard, wrap a flannel cloth around each foot to keep in the heat. Put on woolen socks. The feet should start to tingle and *get very hot.* Tolerance to this heat varies. Wash off immediately if the remedy seems uncomfortable. If the heat is tolerable, keep the plaster on for one to two hours. Go to sleep. This is strong medicine, but today's Ukrainians swear you won't have a runny nose in the morning.

In old Chinese medicine, they also used mustard on the feet. But the Chinese (as well as scores of Europeans) dilute the mustard in a hot foot bath. Here you have two modalities working: hot water and hot mustard. It has the same action as the mustard heel plaster. When fresh circulation patterns start, the healing process begins. DIRECTIONS: Run hot water into a large pan or use the tub. Add two tablespoons of mustard powder. Place the feet in tub or basin for five minutes or so. Wipe the feet. Taking a nap afterwards helps the healing process.

Great trade caravans traveled thousands of miles to bring spices to ancient Egypt. Egyptians used the fennel seed they brought in tea laced with honey to shorten colds. They also added one—or several—of their favorite antiseptic herbs: caraway seeds, anise seeds, cinnamon sticks, or cloves. DIRECTIONS: Lightly bruise "a pinch" of any one of these herbs so that it releases its healing volatile oil, then drop it into a cup of boiling water. Steep, strain out herb, and sip to relieve head congestion and stuffy noses.

Epsom salt baths are a northern European cold remedy. The bath-addicted Europeans liked Epsom salts because it induces profuse perspiration in the bath and immediately afterwards. This, they believed, helps the body discard toxins. DIRECTIONS: Add a cup or more to a hot bath and immerse yourself up to your throat and ears. Reinforce the effect with a small towel around the shoulders. Get out of the bath, and without even drying, wrap yourself in a large bath sheet, and get right into bed. Cover up and sweat off the cold. Do not use Epsom salts if you are pregnant or if you have high blood pressure or heart trouble.

Native Americans taught early settlers in America how to use pumpkin seed tea to conquer mucus from a cold. DIRECTIONS: Cut a pumpkin in half. Reserve the pulp for baking and later eating. Scoop out the seeds. Wash them. Put twenty seeds aside to make tea. Save the rest for additional tea or dry them for snacks. For the tea, boil twenty seeds in two cups of water. Strain and drink as needed.

Bavarians of the last century used the following water remedy. DIRECTIONS: Dip a large towel in *cold* water, wring it out, and place it folded on the chest. Cover the wet towel with a large dry towel. Carefully cover the two towels with a wool blanket. Keep out all air. Leave the pack on for at least half an hour. Because the cold is trapped by the wool blanket, the body will respond to the cold by sending blood to the chest area. Fresh blood circulation breaks up the chest congestion. DIRECTIONS: Duplicate old German herbal vapor baths by running hot water in the shower and/or bath and sitting in the closed room, or plug in an electric steam vaporizer in a small, closed room. These vaporizers are available in drug stores.

Old English herbals have good things to say about the use of peppermint tea as a remedy for an early, mild cold. DIRECTIONS: Pour a pint of boiling water over one tablespoon of dried peppermint leaves. Steep, strain, and drink in small doses over the course of the day.

The Chinese have two points on the body which may help control a cold. DIRECTIONS: Find the hollow behind the lower part of the ear where the neck, jaw, and ear come together. Press deeply. The other point is on the wrist, one and one-half thumbs above the most prominent crease of the wrist, in line with the thumbnail. The point is just below the large part of the thumb—in the hollow.

The Egyptians believed that eating garlic helped to maintain good health. Scholars have translated ancient papyri listing enormous quantities of garlic distributed each day to the Hebrew slaves who built the pyramids. Garlic is a vital antibacterial and can help you confront a cold and conquer any number of other infections. DIRECTIONS: Take the garlic in capsules or, if you enjoy fresh garlic, prepare a huge salad of many crushed cloves plus tomatoes, lettuce, two lemons, and a tiny amount of virgin olive oil. Many colds cannot withstand a garlic attack like this.

If a cold is accompanied by a fever or creates clogging from mucus, people in the mountains of Tennessee traditionally drink catnip tea to lower the fever and reduce the mucus. DIRECTIONS: Pour two cups boiling water over one teaspoon catnip and steep for five to seven minutes. Sip as needed.

All of the Native Americans in North America greatly depended on local plants for prevention and cure of health problems. While each tribe had skilled herbalists, often they used the same plant in different ways. At least fourteen Native American tribes used the purple coneflower to help with colds, coughs, sore mouths, inflammation, and cramps and as a purifier. In particular, the Plains Indians used a Plains species, *Echinacea augustifolia,* for colds and general immunity, sucking on the root all day if necessary to arrest an oncoming cold. About 100 years ago, a German doctor living in Nebraska became interested in echinacea and included it in his successful cure-all patent medicine, claiming it was a blood purifier. Other American settlers learned how to use the plant to forestall respiratory problems such as colds and coughs. But this plant was generally ignored until scientists, mainly from Germany, rediscovered and investigated the plant in this century. Their research indicates that some of its chemical components do stimulate the immune system. And further research seems to show that liquid extracts of the root help fight viral infections. Extracts are available in health food stores. DIRECTIONS: Follow package directions. Take a preventive dose at the first sign of a cold. During the cold, add echinacea to ginger, chamomile, peppermint, or sage tea and sip.

CONSTIPATION

Medical experts are always assuring people that evacuation is a matter of each person's body rhythm. So how do you know if you're constipated? When bowel movements are infrequent and difficult. Dependency on laxatives is not an answer, just an occasional solution. Fortunately, there are innumerable and safe remedies from the sages of the past.

The world's cheapest and most effective constipation cure was discovered by renowned herbalist and hydrotherapist Sebastian Kneipp of Bavaria. His water therapy research established an easy anticonstipation regimen. DIRECTIONS: Drink one to two glasses of *cold* water every morning on arising. Cold water starts peristalsis, the movement of the digestive system that propels matter through it. This simple measure has cured many lifelong cases of constipation.

Another water remedy from nineteenth-century Germany is to drink eight glasses of water per day, along with cleansing juices and herbal teas.

Figs, originally a native fruit of southwestern Asia, were known throughout the ancient world. Early Swiss herbalists claimed that figs were simple, harmless, and effective. In antiquity, the prudent Spartans used figs as part of their daily diet. Their fellow Greeks, the

Athenians, admired figs so much they had laws to prevent fig export outside of their city-state. In Athens, those who informed on the exporters were despised and called *suko phantai* (fig discoverers or fig informers), which evolved into our English word "sycophant." Figs are good natural medicine because the seeds push digested foods through to evacuation. Figs are available in most markets and by mail. DIRECTIONS: For chronic constipation, eat one or two dried figs on an empty stomach each morning.

Aloe is an ancient plant that has been much used for both internal and external healing. It has two completely different abilities: it is a powerful purgative (the strongest of the laxatives), and it is a superb healer of skin bruises and scars. In the fourth century, B.C., several leading Greek doctors cured obstinate cases of constipation with aloe imported from the island of Socotra. The sultan of Socotra apparently maintained a strict monopoly on aloe for many centuries. Fortunately, today, aloe is grown in many places. Juice is pressed from the large leaves and sun dried, then sent all over the world. The pure juice is available in health food stores. DIRECTIONS: Use commercially-prepared aloe juice only on occasion and in small quantities. Check package for specific directions.

Thousands of years ago, the Chinese developed acupuncture, a technique that included the judicious insertion of hairlike needles to rebalance the body's internal *chi*—or energy. Later both the Japanese and the Koreans modeled a noninvasive finger pressure system based on acupuncture meridians, or energy channels. Japanese finger massage is called *shiatsu*; Korean finger massage is named *Gee-Up*. DIRECTIONS: The bony V in the web between the thumb and the index finger influences many body activities, including constipation. If you are constipated, this *Ho Ku* point will feel sore. Press firmly on it and gently rub. Repeat as often as needed. Do not use this point if pregnant.

During the border wars of the twelfth and thirteen centuries, a bag of oatmeal was all that the Scots soldiers carried for provisions. The oat is an invaluable energy food that slowly releases sugar into the system. It also contains bran, a substance that stimulates the intestines and acts in a slightly laxative fashion. DIRECTIONS: To prevent constipation, eat oatmeal each morning, especially the grainier steel-cut oats. An old British recipe for oat gruel combines two ounces of oats to three pints of water. Simmer until the water is greatly reduced. Pour off the water and add raisins or sugar and nutmeg.

It takes the essence of two million flowers (and busy bees) to produce one pound of honey. All ancient cultures used honey for eating pleasure and healing. In the far-away past, when people were closer to nature, various groups of people believed honey helped them to live longer and healthier lives. One old saying is, "Whoever wishes to preserve his health, should eat every morning before breakfast honey and young onions." Early Israelis found honey so important that they regulated who could own bees. Centuries later, the Roman historian Tacitus wrote a book on German tribal customs. He tells us that early German tribes were convinced that their long lives and great strength were a result of mead, which is a beer made from honey. DIRECTIONS: Each morning drink a glass of cold water with a tablespoon of honey on an empty stomach. First add a tablespoon of warm water to the honey to dissolve it, then add the cold water.

The ancient Chinese discovered two foot points to press to overcome constipation. DIRECTIONS: The first point is under the nail of the big toe on the inside near the next toe. The second point is on the inside of the heel and ankle area. Press each area as needed.

The nail-like clove is the flower bud of an aromatic tree. Cloves have been used throughout the ancient world, not only as a spice and a preservative for food, but also as a powerful antiseptic. In tea form, they have been used to encourage sleep and overcome constipation. The Dutch were great admirers of cloves. Several hundred years ago, a Dutch physician described the following remedy to prevent constipation. DIRECTIONS: To release the essential oil, gently bruise about six cloves. Add two tablespoons of hot water to a saucepan and simmer the cloves for about a minute. Add cold water to cover and steep for an additional fifteen minutes. Strain and drink. Prepare each day before breakfast.

Ancient Greek doctors considered the Arab senna plant the most powerful laxative in their plant arsenal. Today, many physicians still prescribe senna before surgical procedures. A standardized senna concentrate is available in an over-the-counter product under the trade name Senokot. DIRECTIONS: Use only as directed on package label.

Before colonialism, Hawaiians had well-trained medicine healers who spent over fifteen years in apprenticeship. They used over three hundred native plants to restore health and spirit among their people. Among the healing tropical plants are many forms of hibiscus, taro root, nightshade, and red pepper plants. One excellent

Hawaiian constipation treatment involves the use of watermelon pulp. DIRECTIONS: For a watermelon fast to cleanse the body of waste materials, try eating dime- to quarter-sized chunks of red watermelon all through the day.

Traditional Chinese healers prescribe frequent doses of rice and ground walnuts for chronic constipation. DIRECTIONS: Each day, prepare eight ounces of rice and twelve walnuts. Soak the rice overnight. The next morning, bring half a cup of water to a boil, throw in the walnuts, and simmer for a few minutes. Grind the walnuts in a blender, add the rice, and rice water. Puree. Take out of the blender and add a pinch or two of sugar and some water. Simmer the preparation until the walnut-rice mixture becomes sticky.

In former times, Chinese doctors prescribed fermented cabbage juice—we call it sauerkraut juice—saying that if it were used once or twice a day, it would produce normal bowel movements in a month or so. DIRECTIONS: Drain and reserve the liquid from a can of sauerkraut. Add an equal amount of water to the liquid and drink. Do not use if you are sensitive to salt or if you have high blood pressure.

CORNS AND CALLUSES

Every culture has experimented with food and plant remedies to soften the layers of thickened foot skin which are the result of repeated and persistent pressure or friction. Hard corns are typically found on the tops of toes where the skin rubs against the shoes, while soft corns form between toes near bone areas. Calluses appear only on the weight-bearing part of the foot, and unlike corns, have no tip or cone.

Tropical island peoples throughout the world used green, unripe bananas to soften corns and calluses. DIRECTIONS: Peel a banana. With a strip of cloth, bandage a piece of unripe banana skin on the callus and/or corn, gummy-side down. Leave it on all night and discard the banana skin in the morning. Apply another unripe skin the next night. Every two days soak the feet in hot water and afterwards scrape away the softened callus or corn. Repeat until all the extra skin is erased.

For over five centuries, the British have been using marigold (calendula) flowers and leaves to heal the skin. In fact, London once had a famous "Marigold Clinic" that specialized in diseases of the feet. DIRECTIONS: To soften the skin, paint the corn or callus with succus calendula or oil of calendula or attach a poultice of the wet pulp of fresh calendula (pot marigolds) every few days.

The early Romans used lemon pulp to remove corns and calluses. DIRECTIONS: Just before bedtime, soak the feet in very hot water and dry thoroughly. Cut off a piece of lemon with the pulp attached. With a strip of cloth, loosely bandage the lemon rind—pulp side down—on the corn or callus. Keep on overnight. Repeat several nights in a row and scrape off the softened callus or corn after each evening's foot soak.

The Scots loved their oatmeal and a long time ago discovered that foot baths in oatmeal water softened hard calluses. DIRECTIONS: Purchase colloidal oatmeal—which is suspended particles of oatmeal—at your local drugstore. Follow package directions and prepare a footbath. Soak the affected foot for ten to fifteen minutes. Pare down softened callus with pumice stone. Continue until corn or callus is erased.

In old New England, they used cranberries on hard corns. Directions: Cut a cranberry in half before bed and apply it to the corn cut-side down. Attach it with a bandaid. Remove it in the morning. Repeat this procedure for one week.

COUGHS

Technically, a cough is a reflex, a sudden noisy expulsion of air from the lungs. It is the body's natural instinct to free the lungs of foreign matter. Natural healers of the past looked upon coughing as the body's attempt to cleanse itself by forcing toxic matter out of an overloaded system.

An excellent example of traditional medicine for a deadly cough was shown in the film *Where the Lilies Bloom.* The film is about orphaned children in the remote mountains of North Carolina. To keep together as a family after their parents die, they hide from authorities and pick wild herbs for a living. One day, they discover a neighbor dying from pneumonia. To save him, they resort to a traditional mountain remedy: a bath of onions. Once he is immersed in the onions, his body weeps out the toxins of pneumonia, and he recovers. Directions: Although onion immersion is a little odoriferous for most of us, similar onion remedies from the mountains include roasting an onion and drinking the squeezed juice or combining cooked onions and honey into a thick syrup. Try either remedy as needed to overcome the most stubborn coughs.

In the latter part of the nineteenth century, Dr. William Fitzgerald experimented with acupuncture points for his ear, nose, and throat patients. He discovered there are points on the tongue and cheek that will relieve coughs. DIRECTIONS: To duplicate the Fitzgerald technique, gently press the middle of your tongue with a tablespoon or tongue depressor for three to four minutes. Repeat as needed in half-hour intervals.

During the filming of his Oscar-winning film, *On The Waterfront*, French cinematographer Boris Kaufman told friends about a cough medicine that had been in his family for generations. "Don't worry that it burns the throat. It stops the cough," his wife Helene assures us. DIRECTIONS: Combine a pinch of ground ginger with ¼ teaspoon of sugar. Put on the tongue just before bedtime and let it dissolve.

To soothe coughs and obstructions of the lungs and windpipe, the Bavarian herbalist Sebastian Kneipp recommended drinking lime blossom (linden) tea. DIRECTIONS: Kneipp employed the tea in two ways—in a steam vaporizer to open nasal passages and as a drink to induce perspiration and discard internal toxins. Purchase commercially available linden tea and prepare according to package directions. Use as needed.

There is probably nothing as effective against a stubborn cough as that traditional European remedy—the chest mustard plaster. It heals by bringing blood to the surface of the skin. This breaks up internal chest congestion. DIRECTIONS: One of the easiest ways to make an old-fashioned European mustard plaster is to combine store-bought (supermarket) mustard powder with enough flour and tepid water to make a paste-like mixture. Add more flour if you want a milder plaster. A normal dose is two tablespoons of mustard powder, plus four tablespoons of flour, plus two tablespoons of tepid (not hot!) water. Construct an "envelope" by folding the paste into a clean, large, man's handkerchief or any soft clean cloth. Apply to the front and back of the chest, as needed. Slide the plaster around to avoid the sensation of burning. For delicate skin, apply olive oil to the skin first.

The Chinese have a fun food remedy for coughs which combines healing honey with either apple or pear. Directions: Make a hole in the side of a pear or an apple. Pour honey into the hole, then steam the pear or apple until cooked through. Mash and eat.

CUTS AND WOUNDS

From earliest times, people have applied a large variety of local plants and foods to stop bleeding and to heal wounds. Primitive cultures learned many common-sense basics for first aid. Among the basics is the washing of wounds and the use of hand pressure to stop spurting blood. (More basic today, of course, is immediate emergency medical care for serious wounds.)

Aloe was a precious commodity during antiquity because its gel healed small cuts. Directions: Break off a small leaf from your own home aloe plant. Slit the leaf open to expose the gummy substance. Smear the gel on the cut. Small cuts should heal within hours.

For centuries, Arabs and northern Europeans applied cut onions to new and old wounds. Directions: A traditional Czech remedy suggests that after cleansing a wound, you chop two onions, toss the pieces into a bowl, add a little salt and some oil, then mix it into a gummy-textured powder. Apply a quarter-sized dollop to the wound and bandage it with a clean cloth. Repeat as needed each day for several days. The villagers who commonly use this remedy advise that the first application stings because the onions eat into the wound and suck out the dirt. They say the pain diminishes after each application and that it is worth the initial hurt for the final quick healing.

Africans, South Americans, and Caribbean islanders often shake powdered cayenne pepper on a wound. This dotting of the wound stings, but the vitamin C-rich powdered cayenne coagulates the blood and quickly forms a healing scar.

People sometimes discover the same healing secret in different parts of the world. In remote areas of China and secluded villages of Europe, for example, they still place paper or wood ashes on wounds to stop bleeding. DIRECTIONS: In a large plate or nonaluminum pot, reduce half of a brown paper bag to ashes. Apply ashes to minor cuts to stop bleeding.

Jamaican islanders use limes for wound control. DIRECTIONS: Squeeze the juice from six limes into a small nonaluminum pot. Simmer the juice until it thickens. Place the thickened juice on a clean cloth and apply to the wound.

The martial arts acupuncture point for severely torn wounds is the *Iang-Koann* point on the fifth lumbar point of the spine. DIRECTIONS: Press the point gently as needed.

In rural Columbia, people place clean cobwebs on cuts and wounds to stop bleeding. DIRECTIONS: Make sure the cobweb is unoccupied, then pull it gently from its supports and apply to minor cuts.

Garlic is a proven effective antibacterial agent. That's why early Egyptians used garlic pounded into vinegar and salt as a remedy for wounds and bloody bruises. During World War II, when the Russian army couldn't obtain antibiotics, they reverted to one of their traditional wound remedies: fresh garlic cloves mashed into powder.

Basil (*Ocimum basilicum*) is a familiar food herb throughout the world. It is even more familiar to the inhabitants of the vast Arabian Peninsula, where it is commonly used for a variety of medicines. DIRECTIONS: In northern Oman and Saudi Arabia, basil leaf juice or crushed basil leaves are placed on wounds to stop bleeding. Wounds are normally then covered with a cloth to prevent infection.

CYSTITIS

Cystitis is an infection or inflammation of the bladder. Cystitis attacks usually start with burning and stinging when urinating. The urge to urinate becomes frequent. The urine can look cloudy or smoky.

Recent American and Israeli research confirms the ancient folk wisdom of using cranberries for bladder infections. Researchers have discovered that cranberries increase the acidity of the urine, and importantly, contain a factor that prevents *E. coli* bacteria from attaching to the bladder or urinary tract walls. DIRECTIONS: Purchase *unsweetened and undiluted* juice and drink at least one pint a day or buy capsules or tablets of concentrated cranberry. Four tablets or capsules are roughly the equivalent of sixteen ounces of cranberry juice. Holistic physicians often recommend the use of two tablets two times a day. Cran-Ute or Cran-Actin are two products occasionally recommended.

A ninety-year-old Finn who has spent all of her adult life healing people with Swedish massage loves to tell about old Finnish, Swedish, and Russian remedies that she's used on her clients. She is a fountain of knowledge on cystitis. DIRECTIONS: Her first recommendation is to slowly sip water throughout the day, but the total amount must be no less than three quarts. You can add lemon juice, cranberry juice, orange juice, or apple cider vinegar to the water. She has seen some stubborn cases cured by adding eight to ten teaspoons of apple cider vinegar to the daily water intake. Here are the rest of her common-sense dictums: don't eat for three hours before bedtime; wear cotton underclothes; change napkins or tampons often; take showers, not baths; be careful that you wipe from front to back when you go to the bathroom; be sure your bladder is empty before and after intercourse.

American black cherry is an old pioneer remedy for those who have pain or trouble with urination. The pure juice is available in better health food stores. DIRECTIONS: Drink it in small amounts throughout the day.

Ancient healers found barley invaluable for urinary problems. The Arab Berbers take water drained from well-boiled and compressed barley, then add honey and lemon juice and take it as a healing drink.

Directions: The French used the following simple remedy for barley water: wash three ounces of pearl barley in cold water, rinse in hot water, then strain. Simmer the barley in two quarts of water. Reduce by half to one quart. Strain and reserve the water to drink. Take a small cupful one hour before each meal and one hour before bedtime.

Several thousand years ago, Chinese physicians discovered they could reach internal organs indirectly by pressing acupuncture points on the skin. Directions: To soothe the kidneys and bladder, lightly massage the bottom, outside edge of each foot along the line of the little toe. Two other acupuncture points are the middle of the tongue and the big toes. Gently press the middle of the tongue with the teeth or a tablespoon, then massage the big toe on each foot.

When research teams study the subject of longevity, they often search for clues in the lifestyle of the vigorous, long-lived Caucasian mountain people and of the nomads of Asian Russia. Investigation shows a key factor in their long lives is their use of yogurt that includes a *Lactobacillus acidophilus* culture. Acidophilus keeps the normal digestive flora active and intact and provides active resistance to innumerable bacterial invasions. The nomads and mountain people have two simple ways to control bladder infections in women. Directions: Women who are prone to bladder infections are told to dab yogurt on the vagina and to also apply yogurt to the vagina directly after sexual contact. This stops the itching and the continuous feeling one has to urinate. Yogurt can also be added to douche water. Check to see if the yogurt you are using is an acidophilus culture. Capsules of acidophilus are available in health food stores.

Traditional Chinese herbalists still use sage leaves and peppermint to control bladder and kidney infections. DIRECTIONS: Combine one tablespoon each of sage and peppermint with two cups of boiling water. Steep, strain, and drink. Take two cups of sage-peppermint tea every day for several months.

DEPRESSION

Depression is a physical state in which one feels unhappy and dejected. Clearly there are degrees to feeling bad. People with major psychological depression—people who feel overwhelmed and unable to cope with their lives—should be under a doctor's care. But sometimes minor depressions are physical, as in a reaction to a low barometric pressure. Other minor depressions can often be overcome with diet, light, and plant remedies.

The bright, cheery yellow flowers of St. John's Wort (*Hypericum perforatum*) have been used by British healers for many centuries for nervous depression and hysteria. Recently German researchers discovered that the use of this herb, especially the oil, can improve one's mood. DIRECTIONS: To prepare a healing tea, pour one cup of boiling water over one ounce of the herb. Steep for five to ten minutes and strain out the herb. Sip one to two tablespoons at a time. To prepare a healing oil, steep a handful of the fresh or dried yellow flowers of St. John's Wort in a pint of olive oil. Add the oil to salads. For depression, some holistic physicians prescribe St. John's Wort in a standardized extract of 300 mg capsules, taken three times a day. Be sure to check for an extract with a listing of 0.125 percent hypericin.

In the past, those who live in northern climates could experience long winter gloom. This gloom made people pessimistic and irritable. They slept more, ate more, and gained weight. Today we have found a name for this syndrome: Seasonal Affective Disorder, or SAD. Researchers claim that people who get SAD are those who may simply need more sunlight than the rest of us. Medical supply stores often sell special light boxes that help overcome SAD symptoms by mimicking sunlight. Still another way to increase light during the winter months is to replace regular light bulbs with full-spectrum bulbs that duplicate sunlight. DIRECTIONS: During the darkest months from December to March, screw in incandescent full-spectrum bulbs over the desk, in the kitchen, and in all reading, craft, and work corners. You can purchase these bulbs through the mail. (See Appendix I.)

When one is nervous or depressed in France, it is an age-old custom to drink "Tilleul," or lime-blossom tea. The lime tree is also called the linden tree. DIRECTIONS: Add a handful of the blossoms to a quart of water, simmer for fifteen minutes, strain, and drink. The honey from linden tree flowers is available worldwide and can be added to the tea for extra calming effect.

Ever notice how exhilarated you feel in the ocean? A group of research-minded nineteenth-century American physicians discovered that adding sea salt or coarse salt to bathwater restored energy. DIRECTIONS: You only need to put about a cup or two of salt in the bathwater to lift your spirits. To further invigorate, use salt as a body friction rub while bathing. Just sprinkle some salt onto a washcloth, then lightly rub it over your chest, shoulders, arms, neck, thighs, legs, and feet. This friction rub discourages depression by boosting internal circulation, giving you a feeling of well-being.

Cloves have had a reputation for lifting the spirits since the days of the trade caravans. DIRECTIONS: Add bruised cloves to any herbal tea during times of depression and gloom.

The Chinese discovered that pressing on the smallest finger of the hand and pressing on the big toes could temporarily lift depression. DIRECTIONS: Press under the inside corner of the nail on the side nearest the other fingers, then massage the big toes. Toe pressure also helps induce sound sleep.

Hungarians have used rosemary as a medicine and cosmetic since at least the thirteenth century. Among the uses they found was as a tea to relieve depression. DIRECTIONS: Simmer a handful of rosemary flowers in a cup and a half of boiling water for ten to fifteen minutes. Since you don't want too concentrated a drink, don't let too much steam evaporate. Steep, strain, and drink.

For centuries, on the first of May, Rhine Germans have produced a Maibowle wine by adding sprigs of woodruff to local wine. The tradition is an old one. Medieval people believed that the highly aromatic woodruff could make them feel better. John Gerard in his 1597 *Herball* says woodruff added to wine "makes men merry."

In earlier centuries, many village healers were sage old women. Often while dispensing their forest herbs, they are said to have practiced an early form of psychiatry by telling gloomy patients they had to smile more. How right they were. Recent research shows that positioning the face muscles into a smile triggers the same positive nervous system effects which occur when people are actually feeling happy and are smiling easily. It seems the body recognizes the smile as a positive signal. The same research reveals that frowns or grimaces or sad, fearful or angry facial movements have a negative effect: heart rate goes up and skin temperature goes down.

DIARRHEA

Diarrhea is the uncomfortable state of frequently passing liquefied bowel movements. The condition can be provoked by bacteria, viruses, stress, or food allergies. Natural healers of the past believed that chronic diarrhea was due to a problem with the general diet, so remedies frequently involved food.

Early Greek and Roman historians mention the use of carrots as medicine. Carrots were first grown in England during the reign of Queen Elizabeth. They were so well-liked that it soon became the fashion to wear the feathery tops in women's headdresses. The carrot was beloved because it was easy to grow, tasted delicious, and had a reputation for preventing internal "putrification." Carrot juice and carrot soup are two old cures for adult diarrhea. DIRECTIONS: To cure diarrhea, even a chronic case, drink two glasses of carrot juice or sip about a pint of carrot soup.

The Greek doctor Dioscorides speaks of the use of "bilberries"—or blueberries (*Vaccinium myrtillus*)—to cure diarrhea. Some consider this one of the most valuable herbal remedies ever discovered. Blueberries are astringent and quickly clear up most cases of diarrhea. Directions: The dose is a handful or more of the fresh or frozen berries three times daily, or half a cup of blueberry juice in the morning and at night. Frozen berries are available year-round in supermarkets. To make a tea of the leaves, use one tablespoon of leaves and simmer in half a cup of water. Strain and drink. You can also purchase bilberry extract in a health food store. Add sixteen drops of the extract to a cup of calming herbal tea such as chamomile or peppermint and sip as needed.

Apple is an ancient cure for diarrhea. Directions: Peel, scrape, and eat. Scraping releases malic acid and pectin—both of which destroy putrefying bacteria.

From time immemorial, people have chewed chunks of charred wood to absorb the poisons that can sometimes cause diarrhea. Directions: Purchase activated charcoal from the pharmacy and use according to package directions. In an emergency, char or burn some bread and eat it to absorb debilitating diarrhea bacteria or viruses.

During a diarrhea attack, it is useful to press the old Chinese acupressure point *Ho Kou*. Directions: Press downward at the web between the thumb and index finger until you touch the bone. Do not use this point if pregnant, as it can bring on uterine contractions.

In the remote reaches of Greece, villagers avoid dehydration from diarrhea with salt, sugar and vinegar. Directions: To each quart pitcher of pure drinking water, the Greeks add one teaspoon of salt, four tablespoons of sugar, and half a cup of apple cider vinegar. They sip several quarts during the day. This is similar to a recipe for severe diarrhea recommended by the World Health Organization, except that the WHO leaves out apple cider vinegar.

Old British herbals usually advise the use of barley water for diarrhea. DIRECTIONS: Wash and rinse one cup of barley. Place in a pint of water and bring to a boil. Throw out the water and start again with fresh pint of water. This time, discard the barley, let the water cool, then drink. This barley water can also be used in a healing enema.

From the early Egyptians onward, doctors attempted to correct diarrhea by first "cleansing" the system with an enema. As drastic as this sounds, it reduces the possibilities of reinfection and rids the intestines of contaminating irritants.

EAR INFECTIONS

Earaches are like toothaches. They can be very painful. Ear infections should be attended to immediately. While many of the remedies of the past act as both a shield and a cure against bacterial and viral infections, it is wise to check painful ear problems with your doctor. Never put fluids in an ear if the ear drum is ruptured.

The conquering Greek army of Alexander respected the wide range of Egyptian medicine. Among the many Egyptian remedies they took back to Greece was oil of garlic for earaches. The antiseptic quality of garlic is easily released in either alcohol or oil, although oil is preferable for the ear. DIRECTIONS: To make oil of garlic, pour some olive oil into a small jar. Choose a garlic "head" with clean white buds. Peel and mince several buds or cloves. Place the minced garlic cloves into the olive oil and cover. Let it stand in some moderately warm place for three days. Strain out the garlic and reserve the oil. Label: "Oil of Garlic," and store in the refrigerator. For earaches, warm one tablespoon. Use an eyedropper to place four to five drops of the oil in the ear or soak a piece of cotton in the oil and place the cotton in the ear. It is important to keep the ear warm. Wind a flannel or wool scarf around the ears and head. If your garlic oil is kept in the refrigerator to avoid bacterial contamination, it may also be used in cooking or in salad dressings.

Chinese acupuncture provides us with several skin trigger points to relieve earache pain and itching. Two of the three points are on the same side of the aching ear. DIRECTIONS: First, grasp the tip of the fourth finger on the side that hurts and hold the pressure for about five minutes. Next, on the side of the aching ear, gently lift the lobe of the ear with one hand and with the other gently massage the area behind the ear in the hollow where the ear and the jaw converge. To activate the third point, press on either side of the spine on the spot where, if you drew an imaginary line along the bottom of your shoulder blades, the line would pass.

An old German country remedy, used throughout Europe, relieves pain with heat and bread. DIRECTIONS: Pound a handful of caraway seeds and set aside. Cut off and throw away the crust of a loaf of rye bread. Tear the bread into pieces, place in a baking pan, add the caraway seeds, and mix together. Moisten the mixture with some whiskey or vodka, or better still, with the caraway liqueur, Kummel. Bake the ingredients for fifteen to twenty minutes at 350 degrees. The bread should be very hot. As soon as it is ready, put the bread into a thin, clean cloth. Apply to the aching ear as soon the skin can tolerate the heat. The bread may be reheated and used again to calm the pain.

We have all heard the wise old adage: "Never put anything smaller than your elbow in your ear." So here's a modification of an old Dutch remedy for swimmer's ear that respects that admonition. DIRECTIONS: Combine equal amounts of apple cider vinegar and rubbing alcohol in a small jar. After showering or swimming, dip a cotton-tipped swab into this mixture, and carefully dab the outside of the canal. Then tilt your head, aching ear side up, and let the mixture work its way into your ear. It will help the water evaporate and prevent the itching that comes with swimmer's ear.

EDEMA

Edema is the presence of abnormally large amounts of fluid in the tissue spaces of the body. It occurs with certain conditions such as heart disease and, in some women, before and during a menstrual period. With other health problems, the kidneys sometimes seem to go on strike and must be stimulated. In bygone times, many plant and water therapies were used to safely liberate fluid from the tissues.

One great healing secret of Europe is the use of the hot sitz bath for encouraging urination. DIRECTIONS: Run a few inches of moderately hot water in the bathtub. Sit for several minutes in the water. Leisurely, full hot baths also stimulate after-bath urination.

Watermelon is a staple food and medicine in Hawaii. One of the ways it is used is to promote the release of stored body fluid and as a mild laxative. DIRECTIONS: Eat small pieces of the red meat of watermelon at ten-minute intervals throughout the day.

The first-century Greek physician Dioscorides suggested fennel tea "for those who can only urinate drop by drop." DIRECTIONS: Buy fennel tea in tea bags or add a cup of boiling water to several bruised fennel seeds. Steep, strain, and drink.

The ancient Chinese pressure point for edema is in the middle of the inside of the knee, just below the kneecap. DIRECTIONS: Press deeply several times.

Centuries before strawberries were cultivated for the market, local British healers discovered that wild strawberries could encourage urination. DIRECTIONS: Strawberries from the local market are almost as effective as wild ones. Buy a pint or two and pop them into your mouth throughout the day.

Back in Transylvania, when they weren't busy with Count Dracula, village healers had a secret remedy for urinary retention: horseradish and beer. Horseradish was an old standby for all manner of urinary problems. Sometimes grated horseradish was eaten "straight" in teaspoon amounts, or, if it was too biting, it was swallowed with peasant bread. DIRECTIONS: Boil a clean horseradish root in a glass of beer, cool for a few minutes, then drink the liquid while it's warm. Drink one cup at a time.

Old British pharmacopeias often recommended spirit of juniper to "carry off the effused fluid by the kidneys," especially if the retention of urine was due to a heart problem. DIRECTIONS: The suggested dose was a teaspoon of the spirit and a glass of water, several times a day. Purchase the spirit (or tincture) through a pharmacy, then follow package directions. Do not use if on medication.

Anyone who has savored asparagus knows how it stimulates the kidneys. The early Romans knew this and used the vegetable to encourage urination, as did the Europeans. For retention of body fluid caused by heart problems, for example, the French prescribed a syrup made from asparagus and sugar. The British, however, preferred to use asparagus as a tincture. DIRECTIONS: Buy tincture of asparagus from botanical sources. Or, to make your own tincture, immerse clean young shoots of asparagus in a pint of vodka. Let it stand in a dark closet for a week to ten days. Discard the asparagus. Use eight to ten drops of the asparagus tincture with a tablespoon of water three times a day.

Pumpkin, squash, and cantaloupe seeds have long been a purely American remedy for retention of fluid. DIRECTIONS: Simmer a handful of seeds in boiling water for a half hour, then strain. Drink several glasses of the remaining liquid each day.

EYE PROBLEMS

Thousands of years ahead of their time, Egyptian doctors, extolled in the ancient world as the "knowers of secret art," discovered there were nutritional causes for many illnesses.

They sagely advised their patients to eat liver, which contains hefty amounts of eye-powering vitamin A. Remember the King Tut statue with its heavy, curved, blue-green eye line? Recent laboratory tests have proven that the eyeliner, worn by men and women alike, destroyed bacteria and discouraged infection-carrying flies that cause blindness.

Native Americans are the source of a rich heritage of healing secrets, including a tea of witch hazel leaves to reduce inflammations, puffiness, eye fatigue, and redness. DIRECTIONS: For quick relief, soak two cotton pads in witch hazel *extract* and apply to closed eyelids. Drugstores carry excellent witch hazel extract under the Dickinson label.

To lift droopy eyes, French women would apply chamomile compresses to closed eyelids. DIRECTIONS: Dip a cotton cloth in cold chamomile tea. Fold the cloth into a size that will fit over the eyes. Place it in a plastic bag. Put the bag on a flat piece of cardboard and place it in the freezer. When a reviving compress is needed, remove the frozen chamomile-steeped cloth from the plastic bag and apply to closed eyelids.

To overcome eye inflammations, German villagers and Spanish farmers alike either flushed the eyes with strained, cold chamomile tea or applied a strong, hot chamomile poultice to the closed eyes. DIRECTIONS: To make the poultice, simmer chamomile flowers for fifteen minutes. Strain and place the soggy flowers in a clean handkerchief or thin cloth. Cool slightly, then drape over the eyes.

To bring sties to a head, European peasants used either a hot poultice of strawberry leaves or strawberry-leaf tea on closed eyelids, or they applied cloths (compresses) dipped in the hot tea. DIRECTIONS: Pour one cup of boiling water over two tablespoons fresh or dried strawberry leaves. Apply tea on absorbent cotton squares or on clean handkerchief or cloth.

Warm milk is an old, reliable eye wash and soother of eye inflammations. Farming families of the past repeatedly applied cloths dipped in warm milk. DIRECTIONS: Wring out the cloth and place over closed eyes.

When simple rinsing of the eyes did not clean out dust and dirt, Russian peasants used frozen white bread. DIRECTIONS: Place several slices of white bread on ice or in the freezer. Several hours later, press one slice of the ice-cold bread on the eyes. Replace with a fresh, cold slice every two hours or so. Except for sleep time, keep up the applications for several days, at which point, the dirt should have disappeared.

In the late nineteenth century, eye, ear, and nose specialist Dr. William H. Fitzgerald developed a personalized version of Chinese acupuncture points. In a monograph to other physicians of his time, Dr. Fitzgerald explains how to relieve itching and congestion of the eyes. DIRECTIONS: Loosely wind a gauze bandage soaked in witch hazel over the knuckle joints of both index fingers. Every hour or so, strongly press the joints with the thumb and index finger of the opposite hand. To relieve the pain of sties, conjunctivitis, or granulated lids, use strong pressure on the joints of the first and second fingers of the hand corresponding to the eye involved. If finger pressure is not strong enough, Dr. Fitzgerald advised winding a fat rubber band on the finger joint. Remove the bands every fifteen minutes or whenever they become uncomfortable. Repeat this procedure on and off until the pain is relieved.

The early Spanish beauties in Santa Fe have passed on this cosmetic secret to repair dark circles under the eyes. DIRECTIONS: Cut strips of either gauze or cotton flannel to fit under the eyes. Soak the strips in olive oil and apply for several hours.

FATIGUE

Fatigue can be overcome with rest and strategies for self-renewal and self-repair. Most ancient cultures discovered natural ways to stimulate and restore the body.

Ginseng roots were discovered many eons ago in the forests of China and brought to the attention of the emperor. The herb had such a powerful action in illness, sexual activity, and the restoration of energy that its use was kept a secret and reserved for the emperor and his court. DIRECTIONS: This once-rare root is now available as a powder, extract, capsule, or tea in health food stores or by mail. Follow package directions.

In the last century, Bavarian herbalist Sebastian Kneipp rediscovered and organized concepts of water therapy. Kneipp achieved great international fame by teaching the rest of the world how hot, warm, and especially cold water could revitalize the body and overcome fatigue. DIRECTIONS: To banish tiredness, focus alternating hot and cold streams of water over your entire body. Always end with cold water.

Another answer to momentary fatigue is an immersion in a long, warm bath. While in the bath, try the old German salt rub to restore energy. Directions: You can purchase inexpensive boxes of coarse salt in your supermarket. In the bath or shower, take a handful at a time and rub the shoulders, arms, torso, thighs, legs, and feet. Salt rubs are invigorating and reviving.

If you are tired, start brushing the skin. The ancient Chinese believed it cleansed the lymph system. Directions: Do this daily for about three months and taper off to once or twice a week. Traditional Chinese use the dried fibers of a gourd which we call loofah, or a softer brush of natural vegetable bristles to sweep the skin. Slightly softer crocheted mitts are available in stores. Skin brushing is done on the naked dry body the first thing in the morning. Gently brush the loofah, crocheted mitt, or rough washcloth in long, steady strokes. Brush the arms from the hands to the shoulders, down the neck and across the shoulders, up the legs from the feet to the hips and buttocks.

Even while Europe was in the Dark Ages, Indian yogis were teaching how the breath can renew health and energy. Following is a simplified version of the energy-restoring alternate nostril breathing procedure. It calms and rebalances the body as it helps to overcome nervous distress and fatigue. As soon as you start this deep breathing exercise, it alerts your body that fatigue is out, energy is in. Directions: Sit quietly for a few moments. Clear your mind of thoughts. Center yourself by focusing your eyes on the end of your nose, then inhale deeply several times. Inhale again as deeply as possible, imagining your body is a bottle and your breaths will fill the bottle from bottom to top. Place your right index finger against your right nostril, holding it securely closed. Close your mouth and exhale slowly through your left nostril as completely as possible Breathe in deeply through the left nostril. Hold both nostrils closed and pause for a moment. Place the left index finger on the left nostril. Exhale deeply through the right nostril. Breathe in deeply through the right nostril. Repeat several times. Mentally imagine that you are exhaling dark blue or dark gray vapors and inhaling pure white vapors.

A long time ago, the Chinese invented jujitsu and judo along with acupressure points to revive the body. DIRECTIONS: For exhaustion, press repeatedly on the *Tchong-Tchou* pressure point. On the topside of the hands, touch the skin where the thumb and index finger meet in a web. Move your finger at this point across the top of the hand to the point between the little finger and the fourth finger, then press. *Tsienn-Iu* is another Chinese pressure point used to overcome extreme physical fatigue. It is located at the edge of the shoulders. Press as needed. DIRECTIONS: For weariness, press each toe several times, then press deeply and knead the bottom of the foot, especially the middle area. For general fatigue, press the calf of your leg and the area directly under the kneecap.

The Early Greeks discovered that concentrated bee pollen granules were an antidote to physical fatigue. DIRECTIONS: Bee pollen is available in health food stores. Follow directions on the bottle.

FEVER

"Small fevers gratefully accepted." This was the unusual sign put up by the young doctor, Oliver Wendell Holmes. Dare we guess that he didn't have enough fevers to manage? At any rate, he changed his career to law and became an outstanding Supreme Court justice.

A normal temperature for most people is 98.6 degrees Fahrenheit, although even this can change with the time of day, exercise, and stress. But should we do something about our temperature if it rises? African tribal healers ignore the fevers of colds and flu, as do many other societies. But once a fever becomes debilitating, all peoples find plants and water remedies to reduce it.

Throughout history, water has been a very helpful agent in breaking high fevers. The nineteenth-century herbalist Sebastian Kneipp felt that drinking copious amounts of cool water and rubbing the body with cold, water-soaked cloths would help bring down most fevers.

The "Cold Friction Rub," as Kneipp called it, has a two-fold action. The cold water cools the outer skin and reduces the fever by evaporation, while friction from kneading the skin invigorates the circulation, which stimulates self-healing. Directions: Make sure the feverish person is in a room without drafts. Uncover only one small section of the body at a time. Dip a washcloth in cold water or cold apple-cider vinegar. Wring out the cloth, and use it to rub every inch of the exposed area. Cover, then repeat this action all over the body, one section at a time.

Historically, many European villagers felt that lemon water lowers fever and is also cleansing, healing, and antiseptic. Directions: Squeeze half a lemon into a cup of cool water. Add a dollop of honey to sweeten and drink as often as possible.

In order to lower fevers, Russian village healers prepared an apple tea. Directions: Peel and cut two apples into little pieces and discard the seeds. Add apple pieces to a pint of boiling water, turn the heat off, and let the mixture stand until the apples soften. Add a teaspoon of honey. Eat with a spoon or blend thoroughly and sip slowly.

Sage, one of the most valued of the old plant medicines, is used everywhere in the world. In China, it was so admired as a medicine that the Chinese would trade three pounds of their black tea for one pound of Dutch sage leaves. In the past, Mexican Indians broke high fevers with sage-tea sweat baths and directed sage-tea steam to the nasal passages to reduce congestions of the chest and nose. Early American settlers from Europe drank sage tea for fever and gargled with sage tea and diluted vinegar. During a dangerous typhus epidemic on the island of Nantucket in 1922, residents of the island used sage tea, which they credit with saving many lives during the outbreak. DIRECTIONS: Sage is powerful. One teaspoon added to a pint of boiling water will make a potent tea. To make a tea without boiled water, add a pint of tap water to a tablespoon of sage and steep in sunlight for a few hours. Strain, then sip. This gives you an uplifting tonic drink. Avoid sage during pregnancy, as it stimulates uterine contractions.

Cayenne pepper is a panacea plant in many cultures. It is used as a safe internal disinfectant, as a disinfectant for food, as a tonic, as a circulation aid, as a heart attack preventative, and as a styptic to halt external blood flow. While it seems odd to use such a sharp, biting herb to overcome fevers, cayenne has a long history in fever control among African and Native American tribes. DIRECTIONS: Prepare a favorite tea such as peppermint, lemon balm, chamomile, or catnip, and add a small pinch of cayenne. The amounts of cayenne should vary with the patient's tolerance for the taste.

Just as syrup is tapped as a cash crop from maple trees, in the Far East they "mine" sago, a popular, starchy cereal-medicine excavated from the trunk of the sago palm tree. Powdered sago is cooked into a nourishing gruel or broth for invalids to reduce fevers. At a recent revival of the classic Indian film, *Pather Panchali*, I was reminded that sago broth is truly important to the rural Indian. The movie depicts a young girl critically ill with a high fever. A Bengali village healer arrives to help the mother. His only instruction? "Prepare sago broth." DIRECTIONS: Sago is available at many oriental markets. Follow package directions.

Eucalyptus globulus was first discovered among the aborigines of Australia who used it in sweat baths to ease fever. About a hundred years ago, the director of the Melbourne Botanical Gardens introduced eucalyptus to the world. It now grows everywhere. Oils extracted from eucalyptus leaves are antiseptic and are able to immobilize a variety of bacteria and some of the influenza viruses. DIRECTIONS: To stimulate perspiration which will help break the fever, add either fresh leaves or a tablespoon of eucalyptus extract to a medium-warm bath.

Prospero Alpina, a very conscientious Venetian observer of sixteenth-century Egypt, wrote that the Egyptians used peppermint-leaf tea to prevent an oncoming fever. DIRECTIONS: At the first hint of a fever, drink a cup of peppermint tea.

The ancient Japanese discovered pressure points to control fever. DIRECTIONS: Massage each thumb, then massage the temples. Massage between the eyes and directly above the nose. Apply an ice cube a few seconds at a time to the fleshy pad of each big toe.

The nomadic Bedouins still use licorice root (*Glycyrrhiza glabra*) as an important fever aid. They boil the licorice root in water for four to five hours, strain out the root, and drink the cooled water. DIRECTIONS: It is safer today to use deglycrrhizated licorice in capsule form. Nature's Herbs and Enzymatic Therapy manufacture excellent chewable tablets which are available at health food stores. Follow package directions. People with blood pressure problems should not use licorice in root form.

Aromatic evergreen needles have been used in medicine since the time of the early Egyptians. An ancient writer describes how juniper oil was used to massage the body as soon as a person felt ill or anticipated a fever attack. The aroma and the oil itself stimulated perspiration. Perspiration was intensified by adding covers to the patient.

The aromatic thyme (*Thymus vulgaris*) plant contains the potent chemical thymol. It was a prized medicine and tonic wherever it grew in the ancient world. Among its many uses, the Romans wrote about using thyme to promote perspiration in fevers. DIRECTIONS: Prepare a tea by combining one tablespoon of thyme and one cup of boiling water. Steep, strain, and drink as often as needed. You can use thyme in cooking but not in therapeutic doses during early pregnancy, as it is a uterine stimulator.

FLATULENCE

Flatulence is the unwanted passing of wind from the lower digestive tract. This surplus air is produced by excessive amounts of air or gases in the stomach or the intestine. Basically, flatulence is a problem of faulty digestion. There are numerous natural solutions, many of them from our ancient past.

What would fresh rye bread be without its caraway seeds? It turns out there is a medical reason caraway was used in bread, cheese, and soups. Caraway seeds are an ancient cure for flatulence. The Egyptians used it first. They went to great lengths to obtain the seeds from the island of Caria (hence caraway) in Asia Minor. In the British Isles, where this herb grows freely even in wild places, an old herbal recommends that caraway should definitely be "in the cupboard of every British housewife to consumath the wind and delight the stomach." It takes about six pounds of seed to make four ounces of the essential oil of caraway. DIRECTIONS: Most old herbals suggest this dose: two to four drops of caraway oil dissolved in one tablespoon of boiled water or dropped onto a lump of sugar. In bygone times, caraway was also a favored remedy in Germany, and there is a delicious German liqueur, "Kummel," made with caraway seed. DIRECTIONS: Sip the liqueur in very small amounts to relieve flatulence or add a scant teaspoon of the liqueur to carminative teas such as peppermint, ginger, or chamomile. If you prefer to make your own caraway preparation, bruise a tablespoon of the seeds, place in a pint of cold water, and let stand for five to six hours. Strain out the seeds. Give a child one to two teaspoons or an adult one to three teaspoons at a time, several times a day.

Denmark, the most southerly country in Scandinavia, was first founded in the tenth century, and was the dominant Baltic power until the seventeenth century. To reduce gas pain, Danish villagers applied wet, moist heat to the abdomen. DIRECTIONS: Bring two cups of water to a boil. Add a pinch of salt and two tablespoons of whisky or brandy. Soak a cloth in the water, wring it out, and apply it to the abdomen while still hot.

Caper is the name of a delicious flower of the caper plant as well as a term for an adventure. The Arabs discovered centuries ago that pickled capers had a two-fold use: they stimulate digestive juices and relieve flatulence. DIRECTIONS: Capers are found in the condiment section of supermarkets. Use them as often as you like. The smaller they are, the more taste they have. And they are a no-calorie addition to pasta, salads, stews, and sandwiches.

Bygone herbalists loved sage and, over time, discovered it had many medicinal uses—including pacifying such digestive problems as flatulence. Sage has been so admired over the centuries that its Latin name *salvere* means "to be well," or "to save." Sage is also a cherished table tea throughout the world and is especially admired in Greece, where you can order it in most outdoor cafes. The Chinese valued it as a tea to remedy stomach problems and weak digestion. And in his early English herbal, Culpeper recommended sage drinks for flatulence, or even a side stitch "coming from wind." Culpeper advised application of warm sage compresses onto the area of the "stitch." DIRECTIONS: Place two tablespoons of sage leaves in a pint of water. Bring to a boil, then simmer for ten minutes. Strain out the leaves. Place a folded dishtowel or washcloth in the liquid, squeeze out the water, and apply the warm cloth to the side, ribs, or stomach.

The aromatic seeds of the anise plant were native to Egypt and were often used as a digestive aid. The plant also grew in Greece and Asia Minor and was admired and used by the Greeks and Romans for digestion.

During the Middle Ages, when anise was finally cultivated in central Europe, the plant was often added to strong laxatives to neutralize spasms and "griping." The French are fond of anise in food and as a digestive aid. DIRECTIONS: An antiflatulence recipe from early Rome combines six bruised anise seeds plus a cup of distilled water. Simmer into a tea, strain, and drink. A good shortcut: add a teaspoon of the French Anisette liqueur to calming chamomile or fennel tea. Drink at bedtime.

We often associate the strength of the Scots with the oat porridge they ate. When faced with bloating from gas, the ancient Scots turned to their favorite cereal food for help. DIRECTIONS: Place half a cup of vinegar in a nonaluminum pot, add half a cup of oatmeal, and simmer until the oatmeal softens. Place the hot oatmeal in a soft cloth and apply to the abdomen.

The ancient Greeks used the essential oil of dill as a "gallant expeller of wind." The original dill first grew in Asia, but has since been cultivated throughout the world as a food and medicine. Since ancient times, it has served as a remedy for dispelling wind and easing windy bellyaches in children. DIRECTIONS: Make dill water with bruised seeds and one cup of boiled or distilled water. Steep for several hours, strain out seeds, and give sweetened to infant, one or two teaspoons at a time. The dose for flatulent indigestion is two to four drops added to a tablespoon of milk or eaten on a sugar cube.

FOOT PAIN

The foot is the most used, mistreated, and neglected part of the body. Possibly because all the weight of the body is on one foot or another when we stand or walk, the foot is prone to many problems. All ancient cultures developed natural treatments to relieve foot pain and strengthen the foot.

The Black Forest of Germany gets its name from the dark firs and pines that cover its mountain ranges. For over two centuries, it has been a favorite hiking destination for tourists. In fact, many innkeepers provide a traditional warm foot bath saturated with the healing essence of Black Forest pine needles to relieve aching feet. DIRECTIONS: To duplicate this remedy, place both feet in a container of warm water loaded with pine needle extract. The fragrance will remind you of winter holidays and the unforgettable aroma of pine forests. Vigorously wiggle your toes and, every two to three minutes, add more warm water. Steep feet for half an hour. Pine needle extract is available in better pharmacies or by mail. (See Appendix I.)

Bunions, which are protrusions on the side of the foot beside the joint of the big toe, can be an inherited misalignment of foot bones or a result of wearing tight, pointy shoes. Such shoes cause the big toe to bend inward. Several hundred years ago, when pointy, tight shoes became the vogue among men and women in the French court, aristocrats paid dearly for this fashion. To this day, French families address the bunion problem with these instructions to make sure their toes stay flexible. DIRECTIONS: Put your feet in a cold stream every day or pour cold water over your feet. If possible, walk in the water and shake each ankle. Then massage the big toe on each foot and press the spot between the big toe and the next toe. Rotate the big toe until you achieve flexibility, then massage the entire area of the inner arch from the big toe to the heel. One last suggestion: holding on to a chair, rise on tiptoes, then lower your heels. Repeat several times, but do not let your heels touch the ground.

 The court physicians of Frederick the Great developed this useful daily exercise to avoid heel spurs. The object is to get more circulation and stretch into the Achilles tendon. Directions: Stand with your feet flat about a foot from the wall with arms outstretched upwards at an angle. Lift and stretch upwards, one foot at a time.

FROSTBITE

In Siberia they say, “Don’t go out on a day your spit can freeze before it hits the ground.” Frostbite is a severe reaction to the cold by the skin and its underlying tissues. Injury is usually limited to the extremities, especially the fingers and toes, but it can also involve cheeks, nose, and ears. See your physician immediately if you suspect you have frostbite.

In old, bitter-cold Russia they learned never to apply warm compresses to an afflicted area directly because it would cause pain and damage. Rather, they applied warmth indirectly above the afflicted tissue. Directions: For a frostbitten hand, soak or apply a compress to the whole arm from the wrist up towards the elbow, instead of from the wrist down toward the fingertips. Keep the hand loosely bandaged in some flannel or wool. And keep in mind the Russian peasant warning, “Never thaw a part which might become frozen again before a final treatment.” This may lead to gangrene and tissue loss.

 Early immigrants to the American northern wilderness were unprepared for the extreme cold. They soon learned that with extreme cold the circulation

slows and can even come to a complete halt. Sensation is lost, white blotches appear, and "dead skin" is the eventual result. Through trial and error, they learned not to rub snow on the affected spot, but rather to flail their arms, scrunch their faces, and jump around to increase circulation and prevent the problem. DIRECTIONS: When frostbite did occur, the immigrants tried various foods on the frozen skin, such as a roasted, cooled turnip poultice; cooked, room-temperature mashed potatoes; or water in which the potatoes have been boiled. For chilblains, many settlers also applied the inner sides of cucumber peelings to the frostbitten limbs.

The aloe vera gel has a long history in healing skin and soothing burns from heat or cold. Aloe was used by the early Greek physician Dioscorides and later by Greek and Arabian physicians. The plant was first found in East and South Africa, but was traded and introduced throughout the world. Most garden stores and flower shops now carry small aloe plants for the home. Recent scientific investigation has found that aloe vera cream (or dermaide aloe cream) speeds the healing of frostbite and burns. DIRECTIONS: Apply pure aloe cream four times a day. If no cream is available, split open an aloe leaf, peel back the edges, and squeeze the thick gel directly on to the injured skin.

The mountain Chinese combine honey and lard for a frostbite ointment. DIRECTIONS: Combine seven tablespoons of honey with three tablespoons of lard. Gently heat together. Place the mixture in jar and label "Frostbite Remedy."

The young African general Hannibal is mainly remembered because he trekked over the snow-capped Alps with elephants. Hannibal came from Carthage, a North African city in an area near modern Tunis. Romans sacked his city and killed his beloved father. Hannibal swore that he would avenge his father's death. Since the Romans could repel his attack if he arrived from North Africa by a southern sea route, Hannibal decided he would surprise the Romans from the north. That meant taking an almost impassable path through the Alps. In 218 B.C., Hannibal took ninety thousand infantry, twelve thousand cavalry, and about thirty-six African elephants through Spain, across the Pyrenees Mountains, into the impregnable and bitter-cold Alps. Herbal legend has it that powdered cayenne pepper was one of Hannibal's survival techniques. Being North African, Hannibal already knew that cayenne pepper tea increased internal circulation and created a sensation of warmth. His second survival technique was a tip he learned by watching the Spanish mountain people who had joined his forces. To prevent frostbite, they sprinkled powdered cayenne pepper inside their boots. This kept them warm.

Far from Hannibal's North Africa, the ancient mountain Chinese used chili pepper (a cousin of cayenne pepper) to prevent frostbite. DIRECTIONS: To make a Chinese *liniment,* steep one or two red chilies in a pint of rubbing alcohol for ten days. Strain out the chilies. Apply *externally* as needed. To make a chili tincture that can be used *internally*, steep one or two red chilies in a pint of vodka in the dark for ten days to two weeks. Strain out the chilies. Add between three to six drops of this tincture to any herbal tea as a gentle aid to circulation.

In the cold reaches of Siberia, they still eat iron-rich liver and/or beet soup to keep them from having goose bumps in the winter time. Recent research has proved the value of this wise old folk medicine. Henry C. Lukaski, a physiologist at the U.S.D.A. Human Nutrition Research Center in Grand Forks, N.D., has learned that the ability to regulate body temperature in the cold may depend on the amount of iron consumed daily. DIRECTIONS: Beets, as well as fish, poultry, and leafy green vegetables are rich in iron. Make them a regular part of your daily diet to help resist the effects of cold.

When the Chinese developed the science of acupuncture, they came to believe that there were several points that could be pressed to increase circulation and warm up the body. DIRECTIONS: To find the first point, tilt your head forward, then find the two cavities just behind the collarbone. Relax the shoulders and press one or two fingers in the cavities to activate the points. If the frostbitten skin is red and shiny, press deeply on the *Tchao-Rae* point above the ankle bone on the inner right side of the foot as well. If the skin is bluish, press deeply above the ankle bone of the *Tchao-Rae* point on the inner left side of the foot.

Chilblains are inflammations of the hands and feet caused by exposure to cold and moisture. In Great Britain, they put great stock in the ability of the local and/or the Spanish onion as a poultice to give relief for the soreness of broken chilblains. DIRECTIONS: Apply roasted onions or onions pounded with salt as needed.

GUM DISEASE

Eating a wide range of vitamin C-rich fruits and vegetables can help you resist most gum problems—many of which develop from fatigue, stress, or a misalignment of the bite. Ancient, natural cures to remedy gum sores are effective and easy to use.

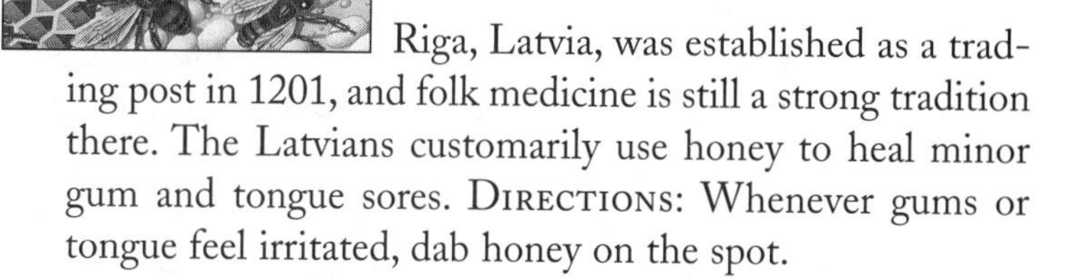

Riga, Latvia, was established as a trading post in 1201, and folk medicine is still a strong tradition there. The Latvians customarily use honey to heal minor gum and tongue sores. DIRECTIONS: Whenever gums or tongue feel irritated, dab honey on the spot.

To control the bleeding gums caused by gingivitis, the ancient Chinese applied pressure on the *Ho Ku* point. DIRECTIONS: To find this point, locate the web between the index finger and the thumb and press. Do not press the *Ho Ku* point if you are pregnant. It can stimulate uterine contractions.

To soothe sensitive gums, the French usually add a tincture or the juice of calendula (*Calendula offincinalis*) to mouthwash. DIRECTIONS: Add pure water to French or Swiss calendula juice. Rinse through the mouth to relieve tender gums. Do not swallow.

To cope with extra-sensitive gums, many Greek villagers traditionally drink mint tea every day. DIRECTIONS: Drink a cup of mint tea. Swish the liquid through your mouth before you swallow.

The Dutch commonly made this egg preparation for sore gums. DIRECTIONS: Break and separate an egg. Discard the white. Beat the yolk together with a tablespoon of olive oil and a teaspoon of sugar. Place the mixture on a piece of gauze, fold, and apply the gauze to the sore gum.

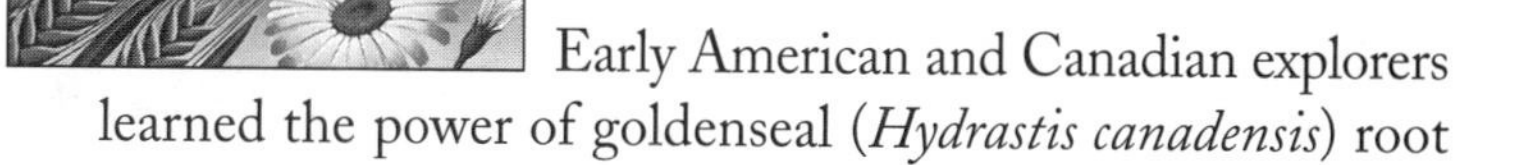

Early American and Canadian explorers learned the power of goldenseal (*Hydrastis canadensis*) root from friendly Native Americans. As they experimented with the powdered root, they discovered it could heal many gum problems, including canker sores. DIRECTIONS: Either apply goldenseal powder directly to the gums or dissolve a teaspoon in a glass of water and rinse through the mouth. Goldenseal powder and tincture is available in health food stores or through mail order sources.

The oleo-gum resin of myrrh (*Commiphora molmol*) has been used since antiquity as an antiseptic by the Chinese, Egyptians, Arabians, and Africans for wound and mouth healing. Myrrh resin, which easily dissolves in oil or alcohol, is generally available in drugstores or health food stores as a tincture. DIRECTIONS: Myrrh is powerful and bitter. You need add only a few drops of the tincture to two tablespoons of water to rinse your mouth. Or use a cotton applicator to apply *diluted* myrrh directly to the sore gum. Do not continue treatment indefinitely, as too much myrrh may be toxic. Do not use myrrh if you have any kidney disease.

The Druids were priests and healers who led the ancient Celtic people of Great Britain and Gaul. We only know of their secret practices through the comments of Julius Caesar and other Romans. The Romans observed that vervain (*Verbena offininalis*) was one of the Druids' most sacred and purifying herbs. DIRECTIONS: Combine two tablespoons of vervain tea with one cup boiling water. Let cool, then use as a mouthwash for soft and spongy gums. Avoid the herb during pregnancy, as it is a uterine stimulant. Many botanical houses carry vervain tea.

For over five thousand years, Chinese doctors have tended to include licorice (*Glycyrrhiza glabra* and *G. uralensis*) in their herbal preparations for control of canker sores. For severe canker sores and mouth ulcers, many nutritionally knowledgeable physicians use a *de*glycyrrhizinated licorice (which eliminates the hormones that elevate blood pressure). The recommended dose of these chewable tablets for canker sores is three times a day, twenty minutes before meals. Tablets are available in health food stores and include products from Nature's Herbs (DGL-Power) and Enzymatic Therapy (DGL). People with blood pressure problems should not use licorice root or licorice candy.

Bilberries (*Vaccinium myrtillus*) or blueberries as they are also known, are an invaluable medicine. In middle Europe, bilberries are prepared as a mouthwash to overcome gum inflammation. DIRECTIONS: Squash some fresh or unsugared frozen berries, add water to make a paste, and apply over inflamed gums. Or add five to ten drops of bilberry tincture to a glass of water and rinse through the mouth.

HAIR LOSS

Normal hair loss is one to two hundred hairs a day. But excessive hair loss—the kind that causes bald patches—is influenced by inheritance, hormones, and excessive stress. Hair, a combination of protein and minerals, responds positively to nutrition, scalp massage, and mental stimulation.

Do-In is a daily stretch-and-touch system originated by ancient Chinese monks. Each day the monks used this system. They worked to achieve flexibility and suppleness with easy stretches, then stimulate mind and body with tapping, rubbing, and massaging of various key points of the body. The combination of Do-In stretches and self-massage invigorates the body and increases internal and scalp circulation, all of which strongly affect hair health and growth. DIRECTIONS: Twice each day, tense the hand and fingertips as if you are holding a ball, then use your fingertips to vigorously tap the scalp all over until it tingles. You can also stretch out on a slant board with your feet higher than your head. This, the Chinese believed, helps hair growth, produces a vital skin tone, and sharpens thinking.

Folks who live in the Ozark Mountains consider red sage a wonderful hair tonic that can also restore the original color of grey hair. Mountain people add about a pint of boiling water to a handful of a mixture of walnut leaves, mullein leaves, and garden sage to produce "the best hair tonic of all." According to local herbalists this combination makes the hair grow and look good too.

In Ayurvedic medicine, rosemary (*Rosmarinus offininalis*) is used to remedy hair loss and to mollify psoriasis of the scalp. DIRECTIONS: Add a handful of rosemary leaves to a pint of boiling water. Simmer for at least fifteen minutes. Strain, cool, and rinse through the hair. Nettle, another excellent scalp stimulant, is sometimes added to this rinse.

Ancient Chinese medical practitioners believed that each finger is invisibly connected to the scalp and that finger massage stimulates the scalp and guards against loss of hair. DIRECTIONS: Rub the fingers of each hand against the fingernails of the other for several minutes at a time, three times a day. You can also help hair health with scalp massage. First, put your left hand palm side down on your forehead. Then use your right hand to move the scalp forward and back. To be effective, this massage technique should be repeated several times a day for months.

Dioscorides, the first-century Greek physician, traveled with the Roman army and observed Romans applying the following onion scalp rubs to halt baldness. DIRECTIONS: Use raw sliced onion, onion steeped in vodka, or onion mashed with honey. Apply any of these to the scalp each evening before sleep. Cover the head to protect your bedclothes. Wash out your hair in the morning.

In the days of the pharaohs, the Egyptians had developed a great skill in the use of herbs, and their herbal traditions were kept alive by the Copts, early Christians who were their direct descendants. The ancient Egyptians used an oil made from seeds of the castor oil plant (*Ricinus communis*), while the Copts employed the root of the plant. The Copts crushed the root in water, allowed it to steep for some time, strained out the root, and applied the remaining water as a wash to the head. Other peoples from the Far East generally applied castor oil directly to the hair as a treatment to halt hair loss and to promote the growth of new hair. Castor oil treatments were sometimes alternated with slathering the scalp with aloe vera juice, olive oil, equal amounts of rosemary tea and olive oil, onion juice, or onion juice mixed with honey. DIRECTIONS: Apply any of these concoctions to the scalp before bed and cover with a plastic wrap to protect the bedclothes. Rinse your hair thoroughly each morning.

In the Far East, there has always been a great emphasis on the spirit, as it influences the mind. In India, in particular, they have developed many mental images to overcome illness and promote health. This imaging was also used to encourage new hair growth. DIRECTIONS: Use the power of positive thinking to restart healthy hair. Start out by closing your eyes and counting backwards from ten to one. This quiets the body and readies it for the imaging. Now, in your mind's eye, see yourself standing at a party or some important event in your life. See yourself as the center of attraction and see yourself with a strong mane of thick, lustrous, long hair, cut exactly as you think it flatters you. Return to these images again and again as part of your campaign to restore lost hair.

To control hair loss, overcome dandruff, and soften the hair, Siberians of previous eras used two agrimony *(Agrimonia eupatoria)* root remedies. One remedy is strained agrimony root "soup;" the other is agrimony soup with cognac and onion juice. DIRECTIONS: Cover one or two agrimony roots with water and boil them until the roots are soft. Carefully strain out the roots. Add about a shot glass of cognac and the juice of one onion, or not, as you choose. Rinse your hair with the mixture every day.

HAY FEVER

For many of us, spring usually means pollen, and pollen spells misery. It causes allergic rhinitis that affects the mucous membranes of the nose, throat, and eyes. Symptoms include itchy or watery eyes, irritability, runny nose, and sneezing. The name "hay fever" stuck to this group of symptoms after a particularly devastating allergy epidemic during the British haying season of 1820.

Horseradish is a plant that has been in cultivation from earliest times and is one of the five bitter herbs used by Jews at the feast of Passover. It was used as a condiment for meats in Denmark and Germany, and in France was known as the "German mustard." Horseradish is a powerful stimulant, and one of its many uses in

Russia, Poland, and Finland was to clear the sinus passages, especially during hay fever season. DIRECTIONS: Combine a few drops of fresh lemon juice with one half-teaspoon of prepared horseradish from the supermarket. Eat at both breakfast and supper.

People with hay fever are especially miserable during certain key months of the year. During these times, they lose a great deal of fluid by sneezing and by a watery discharge through the eyes and nose. DIRECTIONS: Swiss hay fever sufferers were advised to drink at least two quarts of liquid a day—plus raw vegetable juices that included beets, carrots, celery, cabbage, parsley, and other greens.

The predisposition to allergies runs in families, and, in the farming areas of Rumania, residents recommended long regimens of soured milk or yogurt for victims of "hay fever." It was generally believed that a cup to a pint of yogurt a day reestablished the proper flora within the intestines and that this in turn made patients resistant to outside contaminants.

The early Greeks were keen on a food combination they called "oxymel," which is a mixture of equal amounts (from a teaspoon to a tablespoon each) of apple cider vinegar and honey added to a cup of water. This combination tastes like perfect apple juice, and, when used consistently prior to any allergy season, it helps to protect the individual from many allergic reactions. DIRECTIONS: Drink several glasses a day for two to four weeks prior to the allergy season. Beekeepers worldwide recommend eating honeycomb for at least a month prior to the allergy season to desensitize people to pollen.

Hay fever attacks often lead to further misery in sinus attacks. To offset the pain of such an attack, villagers in southern France prepared a unique milk and onion remedy. DIRECTIONS: Scald a cup of milk and drop in one tablespoon of grated onion. Drink while still warm to clear the nasal passages as needed.

Even in the clear mountain air of Macedonia, villagers needed remedies for allergy relief at certain times of the year. To control and relieve nasal congestion during those times, Macedonians eat a clove of garlic every six hours during the day.

HEADACHES

Headaches can vary in cause and intensity from mild tension to searing pain. Stress and other causes make the muscles of the face, neck, and head contract. This contraction reduces blood supply and produces pain. Down through the centuries, every culture developed a wide variety of water treatments, plant remedies, and pressure-point therapies to treat headaches.

About twenty-five hundred years ago, Darius the Great ruled over the powerful Persian empire that spread from the Aegean Sea to the Indus River. Darius built roads as well as the first known post houses—places for travelers to stay as they traveled his kingdom to trade. Understanding the tense rigors of the road, the posthouse offered its visitors hot, wet compresses for their headaches. The Persians knew wet heat applied to the head relaxes painful scalp muscles and speeds fresh circulation to constricted areas. This ancient Persian remedy works for today's headaches, too. DIRECTIONS: Fold a small towel until it is several layers thick. Dip it into very hot water. Wring the towel out and apply it (as hot as is comfortable) to the neck and temples. Keep the heat in by covering the wet towel with a slightly larger dry towel. Place new hot towels to the neck and temples every five minutes to achieve relief.

For headaches, many Hungarian villagers long ago made a conserve or jam of rosemary and sugar. DIRECTIONS: Combine fresh tops of rosemary with three times their weight of sugar. Use a teaspoon at a time in rosemary, clove, or woodruff tea.

In Hawaii, *Awapuhi kuahiwi*, which we call ginger root, grows wild all over the islands. Hawaiian healers relieved headaches by applying ginger root juice or pounded root and coarse salt to the head. DIRECTIONS: Cut a piece of ginger root and squeeze out some juice. Apply it to any part of the head that hurts. Ginger root is available at oriental grocery stores and by mail. (See Appendix I.)

Describing a system of finger pressure based on Chinese acupuncture points, the American doctor William Fitzgerald wrote nearly a century ago, that "Headaches and neuralgias of purely nervous origin . . . usually subside under this pressure within a few minutes." According to Fitzgerald, the hands are a microcosm of the entire body. He divides the body into ten zones which correspond with the ten fingers. DIRECTIONS: To find the zone controlling a headache, put the hands up to the face, palm side facing away from your body. This means the thumbs are near the nose, and each pinky is at the extreme outer edge of the face near the ears. *The finger over each zone influences that zone.* If the headache is in the center or near the eyes, for example, you will press the joints of both thumbs. If the headache is at the edge of the left side of the head, press the left pinky. With the finger of the opposite hand, deeply press the *two* joints of the finger or fingers that correspond to the area of the pain. (You can never go wrong by pressing an extra joint or two.) The most important factor is the extent of the pressure. Fitzgerald advised winding fat rubber bands over each of the finger joints if you haven't accomplished headache relief. Unwind after a few minutes or if it's uncomfortable. Repeat this winding and unwinding of the rubber band over the same and other joints until the pain disappears. People with circulation or heart problems should avoid this technique.

This simple foot bath relieved resistant headaches in many European villages. Foot baths divert congestion from the head by drawing the blood to the feet. This immediately eases many headaches. DIRECTIONS: Run hot water into a basin or in the tub. Use one of the following in the water: A tablespoon of essence of pine, four tablespoons of strong thyme tea (thyme is also an old Egyptian headache remedy), or two tablespoons of powdered mustard seed. Check to see that the water isn't too hot, then place your feet in the water for five to ten minutes. The fatigue and tension that can cause a headache will usually disappear.

Early Greek physicians utilized at least two types of mint for headaches. By the eighteenth century, the plant had worldwide use as a stimulating tonic. DIRECTIONS: To prevent headache pain in ancient times, the Greeks recommended drinking peppermint tea each morning and evening. They also found that binding the wet tea leaves in a cloth to lay across the forehead during a headache eased pain. Later during the Renaissance,

Italians sometimes stuffed a fresh mint leaf in the nose to cure a headache.

The Appalachian herbalist Tommie Bass speaks of catnip as having a "loud odor," and recommends it highly as a remedy for headache and insomnia. DIRECTIONS: For adults, combine three to four tablespoons with a cup of boiling water. Steep, strain, and drink.

Throughout Europe and the Near East, the leaves and flowers of sweet basil (*Ocium basilicum*) are used as a nerve tonic and stimulant. For headaches, the ancient Egyptians sometimes used basil, but if they didn't have basil, they substituted marjoram. DIRECTIONS: For headaches from nausea or vomiting, crumble a handful of fresh basil or two tablespoons of the dried herb into a cup of boiling water. Steep, strain, and drink as needed. Or make the tea and add two tablespoons of witch hazel extract. Then soak a cloth in the mixture, wring it out, and apply as a compress to the forehead and temples.

To offset headaches, especially those due to eye strain, ancient Indian Ayurvedic doctors recommended massage and firm pressure to the nose, eyebrow, and temple area. DIRECTIONS: Place the tips of both index fingers at the tip of the nose. Stroke up the midline of the nose to the top. With both fingers, pinch the area between the eyebrows. Apply gentle to strong pressure under and above the eyebrows, first on the right side, then the left.

Chinese pressure points were developed several thousand years ago and are still in use today to relieve headaches. DIRECTIONS: For general headache, pinch the skin between the eyebrows between your index finger and your thumb. Then pinch the skin in the midline of the back of the neck. For a stress headache, apply pressure on the crease of the inner wrist in line with the smallest finger. Use the right or left hand depending on where the headache originates. For stress headaches on the top of the head, apply deep pressure on the center bottom of the feet, just under the padded part. For migraine headaches, deeply press the *Ho ku* point on the bone at the edge of the web between the index finger and the thumb. Then, with two thumbs, deeply press the point at the top of the neck in line with the ears, just on either side of the center of the skull.

We modern people love instant relief for headaches, so it is interesting to find an old Siberian remedy which is praised for relieving a headache in two hours. DIRECTIONS: Pound one large onion and mix it with two pinches of coarse salt and one teaspoon of olive oil. Put this onion paste on a cloth and drape it over the area that hurts. The paste will draw out the pain.

Sage is a remarkable and versatile healing herb, used throughout the world as a tea and medicine. The Danes combine sage and egg for a traditional headache remedy. DIRECTIONS: Cook a handful of sage leaves in water until they get mushy and sticky. Mix them with one beaten egg and apply directly to forehead and temples.

The Umeboshi salted plum is one of the oldest healing secrets of the Japanese people. Modern studies show that the ume plum alkalinizes the bloodstream and thus rebalances the body. The present-day Japanese use ume pickled plums to prevent a wide range of health problems, and many believe that the eating of this plum influences longevity. DIRECTIONS: For headaches, the ume is used in two ways:

as a plaster to the temples and as a food medicine. Purchase umeboshi plums and plasters at oriental markets, in select health food stores, or by mail. Follow package directions.

The Egyptian Copts had high praise for the oil they extracted from the castor bean, particularly as a compress for headaches. An ancient papyrus says to "Place it on the head which suffers, the patient will soon feel as well as one who is not ill." DIRECTIONS: Purchase a reputable, deodorized castor oil. It can be used for other healing techniques. Soak a small, clean cloth in it, drain the cloth, and apply to the forehead.

Horseradish is a stimulating herb when eaten internally and brings blood to the surface of the skin when applied topically. To cure a headache, the Finns utilized horseradish's ability to draw blood from other parts of the body. DIRECTIONS: Grate some horseradish and apply in a cloth or gauze bandage to the bend of the elbow and the back of the neck.

HEARTBURN

Heartburn may be one of the oldest and most common health problems in the world. Scientists estimate that ten percent of the American people suffer from it every day. It's a burning sensation in the chest which occurs when an excess of stomach acid is regurgitated up the esophagus toward the throat.

In the fifth century B.C., the powerful Persian Empire attempted to conquer the small city-states of Greece. The struggle lasted twenty years. During this period, King Darius I of Persia worked closely with a favored general who often complained about the acid "burn" in his chest. Darius ordered his personal physicians to solve his general's problem. Their advice? The general was ordered to sleep on an inclined bed with his head higher than the rest of his body. Directions: This is also the advice modern doctors frequently give to people with heartburn. Raise the head of the bed by placing four-, six-, or even eight-inch wooden blocks, bricks, or fat phone books under the legs at the head of the bed. Elevation is an effective mechanical aid to deter acid slipping up the esophagus during sleep, but make sure the bed is steady before you get in. Some people have found it safer to drill a hollow in the blocks in which to place the bed's legs.

The flower buds of the clove tree have been used for food preparation and medicine since antiquity. A long time ago in Holland, cloves were used to help heartburn patients sleep longer and better. Directions: Gently pound about half a dozen clove buds to release their oil. Simmer the cloves in a cup of water for ten minutes, then reduce the water by half. Strain out the cloves, add additional water to taste, and drink the liquid.

European village healers advised people with heartburn to drink plenty of water to flush out the esophagus. Directions: Drink at least one glass of water after every meal.

Italians have always loved, admired, and used lemons for cooking and medicine. Directions: If the heartburn you usually get is not from eating sweet things, cut a lemon into thin strips and dip the lemon into salt. Eat one strip before each meal.

The consumption of almonds during the Middle Ages was prodigious. In 1372, an inventory by the queen of France's staff lists five hundred pounds of almonds but a scant twenty pounds of sugar. Almonds have an oily constituent which helps to relieve heartburn. DIRECTIONS: In Central Europe, patients were directed to "to peel and eat six or eight almonds" to lessen heartburn symptoms.

Angelica (*Archangelica offininalis*) has a long history of medicinal use in Europe. In East Prussia, the plant is still a part of a rural spring chanting ritual that goes back to pagan days. The roots and leaves and angelica's medical use are lauded in Parkinson's 1629 herbal, a book in which he also stressed its ability to control flatulence. DIRECTIONS: Most ancient and modern herbalists recommend the seeds of angelica for heartburn problems. Crush one teaspoon of angelica seed and add to one and a half cups of cold water. Bring to a quick boil, reduce immediately, and simmer for fifteen minutes. Strain and drink the tea.

HEART PALPITATIONS

"Two things are bad for the heart: Running up stairs and running down people," said the late financier Bernard Baruch. History records some interesting preventive and emergency approaches to heart troubles. All bear knowing, but since irregular heart rhythms can be fatal, a doctor should be immediately consulted should *any* heart symptoms occur.

In past centuries, the British employed lemons and lemonade to sedate and "allay hysterical palpitation of the heart." DIRECTIONS: Wash and scrub four large lemons. Boil a quart of water and let it cool. Squeeze the juice of three large lemons into the cool water and add several crushed strawberries. Cut up one of the scrubbed lemons and add the rind to the lemonade. Mix and sip whenever you feel upset.

Herbalists of many cultures ardently believe that the sharp, biting, powdered cayenne pepper is one of the most benign and useful of the medicinal herbs. Mexican Indians place a pinch of powdered cayenne pepper on the middle of the tongue as a traditional remedy to arrest a heart attack.

A Mormon midwife, familiar with alternative medicine, demonstrated the following Chinese massage point to avert a heart attack. She had learned it from a family of Chinese descended from those who built the transcontinental railroad. DIRECTIONS: Vigorously massage the pinky of the left hand. Gently tap and pat upwards along the line of the pinky to the wrist. Move up the wrist on the line of the pinky to the elbow. Lift the left hand and arm upwards with palm side inside facing the body. At the lifted elbow, cross an imaginary line at the chest and across the chest to the area of the heart.

Hawthorn (*Crataegus oxycantha*) is a venerable heart-easing herb. Current research shows parts of the herb enhance blood and oxygen supply by dilating coronary blood vessels. To improve circulation and to act as a tonic for heart problems, western herbalists recommend hawthorn juice and/or tea made from the flowering tops and berries of hawthorn. In Europe, present-day physicians often use hawthorn extracts combined with magnesium and other vitamins to improve general cardiac health and decrease angina attacks.

Calendula offininalis (pot marigold) was used in the sixteenth century by the herbalist Culpeper to "strengthen the heart." The dose was two or three flowers eaten raw in salads or two teaspoons of the petals steeped in a cup of boiled water as a tea. *The Herball or Generall Historie of Plantes* of 1597 recommends a conserve of calendula flowers and sugar, noting that a conserve "taken in the morning fasting cureth the trembling of the hart."

Early settlers to America discovered that the bark of the American wild cherry (*Prunus virginiana*) would not only halt a hacking cough, but could quiet nervous palpitations of the heart. DIRECTIONS: Use a cherry bark extract, tincture, or preferably syrup. Either add ten to sixteen drops of the tincture or extract to water and drink or add a teaspoon of the syrup to two tablespoons of water and sip the sugary water every few hours.

The ancient Romans knew certain principles in the asparagus acted on the kidneys and encouraged elimination of stored fluid. Furthermore, they learned that their beloved asparagus also could calm heart palpitations. Centuries later in Great Britain, the shoots were pounded into a powder, and a small, infinitesimal amount of the powder (one grain or 0.065 of a gram) was given three times a day to relieve the edema from heart disease.

HEAT EXHAUSTION

Some folks thrive when the weather is wet with humidity and sizzling hot. Others are overcome by heat exhaustion or heatstroke. Caution is the guide here, so when a person is overcome by the heat, get them instantly cool and wet—

fans, wet sheets, cool baths—the works, and have them recline with their feet elevated. If that person's temperature rises above 103 degrees, request immediate professional help.

Water drinking and splashing acts as a shield against temperature changes. And in the summer, water protects against overheating. DIRECTIONS: During heat waves, drink at least eight glasses of pure water and lightly salted lemonade each day to quench thirst and stay cool. Also stay cool with frequent showers, dip wrists and/or ankles in cold water, or apply wet, cold compresses to forehead, back of the neck, wrist, and ankle.

Originally the people on the vast Arabian Peninsula were separate tribes, but in the seventh century, they were united by a common religion, Islam. Watermelon first grew wild in this region, and it has long been used to maintain coolness and prevent heatstroke. In fact, followers of Islam often start their month-long fast of Ramadan with chunks of watermelon. DIRECTIONS: Eat watermelon frequently throughout hot weather.

The ancient Romans had a neat trick to divert the heat and excessive humidity of hot Roman summers. To prevent the harmful effect of the heat, they tucked a spray of pennyroyal (a member of the mint family) behind each ear.

The pineapple was first found growing wild in the West Indies and South America. While the most valuable healing factor in pineapple is its similarity to human gastric juices, which makes it (and its enzyme bromelain) indispensable for digestive problems, the Carib Indians drank fermented pineapple juice to relieve body heat in hot weather. DIRECTIONS: Sip ice-cold pineapple juice throughout hot weather. Or freeze undiluted pineapple juice in ice cube trays and add to other beverages and juices.

During the nineteenth century, observant natural healers discovered that patients overwhelmed by heat actually cooled off and recovered faster if they were first enveloped in a wet sheet and then massaged through the sheet. DIRECTIONS: Drench a sheet in cold water, wring it out a bit, quickly wrap it around the heat-afflicted person, and proceed to vigorously massage the body through the sheet. At the same time, apply cold compresses to the head and heart area. Renew the cold sheet and compresses every fifteen minutes.

In ancient times, the Chinese used breath to expel unwanted heat from the body. DIRECTIONS: Calmly breathe in and out several times as you normally do. Then breathe in through the nose and expel the air through the mouth saying "Chway." Repeat as needed.

Desert Arabs not only find the stain of henna attractive on the body and hair, they also apply henna to the soles of the feet and palms of the hands to keep themselves cool. Henna is also used to soothe heat-related swollen ankles and scorched feet as well as burns and blisters. DIRECTIONS: Steep two tablespoons of henna in a pint of apple cider vinegar. Soak a cloth in the vinegar. Wring it out and apply to the head to alleviate headaches and other pains caused by excess heat. Unfortunately, it will also stain the skin.

Elderflower is a traditional British and American herb choice for sunburn, heatstroke, and heat exhaustion. The *Practical Housewife*, published in 1860, says elderflower ". . . is the mildest, blandest, and most cooling ointment which can be used, and is very suitable for anointing the face or neck when sun-burnt. It is made of fresh elder-flowers stripped from the stalks, two pounds of which are simmered in an equal quantity of hog's lard till they become crisp, after which the ointment, whilst fluid is strained through a coarse sieve." DIRECTIONS: To purchase excellent elderflower lotion, check out the mail-order catalog of Caswell-Massey.

Lemon fruit and lavender flowers each smell like a clean, breezy summer day. The lemon is not only aromatic, its juice is cleansing and thirst-quenching. In the old American South, homemakers added water to lemon juice and sugar for a cooling lemonade. A small amount of table salt was sometimes added to the drink to replace the salt that evaporates through perspiration. In the summer, Britains preferred the cool, clean aroma and fragrance of cold lavender tea. DIRECTIONS: Steep a handful of dried lavender flowers in about three ounces of boiling water. When the color and aroma emerge fully, strain out the flowers, and add a quart of cold water. Place in refrigerator to cool.

Here are two Chinese skin points to press in times of excessive heat. DIRECTIONS: To counter the effects of the heat, deeply press the point under the nostrils, in the middle section above the lips. Also press hard just below the foot's metatarsal pad, in the center of the sole.

Homeopaths often have simple, safe, and effective answers to emergency problems. DIRECTIONS: To make a faster recovery from heatstroke, homeopaths recommend ingesting three 12x tablets of Natrum mur. with every half-cup of liquid and alternating the dose with 12x tablets of Ferrum phos. with every half-cup of liquid.

HEMORRHOIDS

About one in three Americans suffer with a painful varicose vein in the rectum, which is generally called a "hemorrhoid" or "piles." The problem is aggravated by low-bulk diets, which in turn cause constipation and straining. (See also Constipation.) Standing too much and pregnancy are other contributing factors to hemorrhoids. In the past, there was more of an attempt to get at the cause rather than the symptom of this problem. Thus, village healers concentrated on eliminating constipation and advised walking and stretching exercises to overcome the sedentary lifestyle which contributed to it. The following are ancient healing remedies that alleviate the discomfort and pain of hemorrhoids.

Every village and city in Europe has water remedies for hemorrhoids. These water treatments originated in nineteenth century Germany. DIRECTIONS: Apply ice packs to stop bleeding. Apply cold compresses on the area between the anus and scrotum or vagina to stop any bleeding. For general pain, sit for five to fifteen minutes in about five inches of warm bathwater. Dissolve half a cup to a cup of cornstarch in the water to relieve itching. Then apply hot compresses to the hemorrhoids for fifteen minutes, five or six times a day.

The art of grinding sesame seeds into a food "butter," called tahina or tahini, was a secret Mesopotamian recipe which was learned by the Egyptians and passed on to other Near East cultures. Although tahini was mainly used as a food, ancient Egyptian medical papyri mention it also as a healing unguent for hemorrhoids.

Swedish village healers apply this traditional green onion salve to enlarged hemorrhoids. DIRECTIONS: Finely chop two cups of green onions. Simmer the onions until they're soft. Quickly add two tablespoons of wheat flour and half a cup of cocoa butter. The cocoa butter will melt quickly and create a salve-like texture. Place the hot mixture in a soft cotton cloth (an old clean handkerchief would be excellent) and apply overnight to the area of the hemorrhoid. Repeat for several days to accomplish relief. In Great Britain, healers prescribed roasted onions or onions pounded with salt directly on the hemorrhoids to relieve the pain of piles.

Native Americans discovered a wide range of medicinal uses for the liquid extracted from witch hazel twigs. Witch hazel, which is now available in purified extract form, can help relieve inflammation and stop bleeding. DIRECTIONS: To constrict and shrink engorged veins, apply cloths dipped into cold witch hazel. Or combine the best quality witch hazel, such as Dickinson's, and cocoa butter. Shape into cigarette-shaped suppositories. Freeze in separate pieces of aluminum foil. Remove foil and apply as needed. There is also a witch hazel product, Hamamelis, for hemorrhoids that are large, sore, bruised, and bleeding. Hamamelis is also available as a hemorrhoid ointment.

Amish folk medicine provides this practical tip to eliminate hemorrhoid pain. DIRECTIONS: When going to the bathroom, wipe only with wet, warm tissues. Blot the area with soft, dry tissues. A modern alternative to wet, warm tissues is to use a spray bottle of warm water on the area. Blot dry with soft tissues.

The word myrrh is familiar to us as an incense. The word comes from the ancient Hebrew and Arabic word "murr," meaning bitter. Myrrh has been a valued antiseptic, wound aid, and aromatic medicine. For thousands of years, Arab traders had a monopoly on its sale and distribution. They cleverly protected their source of myrrh (as well as the equally valued cinnamon, cassia, and frankincense) with ingenious, outrageous, tall tales. Even the fearless Greeks and Romans believed the Arab stories of winged snakes protecting spice trees and the huge dinosaur-like birds that had to be diverted from the cinnamon tree. DIRECTIONS: Buy a tincture of myrrh from your local drugstore. Add five drops of the tincture to a cup of water. Shake and apply on a soft cloth to the hemorrhoid. Avoid in pregnancy, as myrrh is a uterine stimulator.

Early European Crusaders to the Holy Land used two healing herbs: comfrey and St. John's Wort as a salve to alleviate the pain and itch of hemorrhoids. DIRECTIONS: Add three cups of boiling water to a handful of chopped comfrey and St. John's Wort leaves. Cook for twenty minutes. Strain out the water. Add the soft leaves to several tablespoons of cocoa butter and simmer together for ten minutes. Put into a labeled jar and store in the refrigerator. Apply this unguent to the hemorrhoid, then carefully wipe off after an hour. It can be repeated as needed.

Throughout history, various muds and clays dug from the earth have been used for internal and external healing. Neutral clays such as bentonite and the French green clays have been successfully applied to hemorrhoids. Directions: Purchase green clay powder in a health food store or by mail. Mix two tablespoons of clay, half a teaspoon of water, and a tablespoon of witch hazel extract into a thick paste. Add more clay if it is runny. Apply directly to hemorrhoids or as a poultice on a handkerchief. Leave it on until it dries and gets flaky. Wash off in shower or tub.

On Caribbean islands, residents apply the gel from an aloe leaf to heal hemorrhoids. Directions: Slit open a small aloe leaf from your windowsill plant, squeeze out some healing gel, and smear it on any hemorrhoids. Repeat as needed. Test a small amount on your hand first, just in case you're allergic to aloe. Don't use it if any redness or irritation appears.

Thousands of years ago, enterprising merchants traveled through deserts and mountains on the old Silk Road to trade with the isolated Chinese. The traders brought spices, rare foods, carpets, and oils and exchanged them for woven silk cloth. The process of silk manufacture was a closely held secret for centuries. The Chinese wrapped gossamer silk thread around engorged hemorrhoids which killed the blood flow to the area and slowly reduced the hemorrhoids until they fell off. Ironically, this ancient healing secret is being safely repeated today by surgeons who find it is a successful, noninvasive "surgery" for hemorrhoids. Surgeons band each hemorrhoid neck with thin surgical thread or a tiny rubber band. This stops the blood flowing and lets the hemorrhoid clot. After approximately a week, the band cuts through the neck of the hemorrhoid, and it disappears with normal bowel activity. This banding should only be done by a surgeon.

Cranberries were presented by friendly Native Americans to the early Pilgrims as a goodwill gift. Cranberries became an honored food and medicine, used to fight infections and urinary problems and to alleviate the pain of hemorrhoids. Directions: Crush some fresh, or unsugared frozen cranberries and place on soft cloth. Apply directly to hemorrhoids.

When hot water is added to sage seeds, they become soft and healing. In Oman, Bahrain, Kuwait, Saudi Arabia, and Yemen the seeds are softened, then applied as a hot poultice for painful hemorrhoids. Directions: Soften two tablespoons of sage seeds in two tablespoons of boiling water. Mash together. Place mash in large clean handkerchief or soft cloth and apply hot to area of pain.

HICCUPS

Most people get hiccups once in a while. There must be hundreds of cures for these involuntary spasms, which often go away spontaneously. Most of the following old remedies work because they shock the system into going back to the normal rhythm of breathing. Notice how many include some action on the tongue and inside of the mouth.

Norwegian villagers liked to use sugar dribbled into the back of the throat to stop hiccups. Directions: Swallow a spoonful of white sugar. Allow the melting granules to trickle down the back of your throat. The sugar works on the nerve endings, and this interrupts the spasms. This same remedy recently turned up in an American medical journal.

Vikings restlessly roamed the world from the early time of Christianity to the time of the Crusades. Everywhere they went to the east, south, and west, they were the agents of European expansion. Later they took perilous land trips to trade from fair to fair. In the late seventeenth century, someone wrote about the best-of-all hiccup remedy—"from a Dane." It requires a clean cloth, no mean achievement in those days, but more than possible today. DIRECTIONS: Grasp the tongue in a clean handkerchief and pull it forward, squeezing it firmly. At the same time, slowly and silently count from one to one hundred. These two actions apparently inhibit the entire zone in which most hiccups start and halts the hiccups.

The early American settlers had an easy approach to hiccups and just recommended drinking something while holding the breath. This helps the breath get back into sync with the lungs.

In the Ozark Mountains, descendants of old settlers pass on this hiccup cure using reconstituted dried apples. DIRECTIONS: Place four teaspoons of dried apples in a cup of water. Bring the water to a boil, stirring occasionally. Strain out the apples, drink the juice while pleasantly hot.

The Chinese hiccup-control center is in the center of the body, immediately below the bottom of the breastbone in line with the navel. Find a sensitive point and press. The Chinese also discovered that the center of the roof of the mouth could be irritated to stop hiccups. DIRECTIONS: Rub the roof of the mouth with a cotton swab at the point where the hard and soft palate meet. This apparently overstimulates the nerve that triggers hiccups, causing it to shut down and stop the hiccuping. Do not use this point if pregnant!

The *Complete Herbal* of 1652 advises soaking and simmering dill in wine, placing it in a cloth, and sniffing it to cure a hiccup. "Dill will stay the hiccough being boiled in wine, and but smelled onto, being tied in a cloth."

Pliny recorded that in ancient Rome they cured hiccups by drinking small amounts of raw cabbage in vinegar (which sounds like Roman sauerkraut) with a little dill added to it. While the vinegar is the irritant that apparently stops the irritated cough, dill must also have some profound aromatic effect. Latter-day Poles favored a vinegar cure. It sounds drastic, so only use it when all else fails. DIRECTIONS: Make a paste of powdered mustard and table vinegar and cover up about a third of the tongue with this paste. Hold it on the tongue for a few minutes, then rinse out your mouth with lukewarm water. Polish scribes write, "The hiccups will stop instantly, sometimes even before the washing of the mouth."

Simple water hiccup cures are legion. Most involve drinking water from a glass at some odd angle. Local Italian village healers advised the following remedy for simple (meaning uncomplicated) hiccups. DIRECTIONS: "Drink a glass of water, but not in the usual way. Drink from the farthest side of the glass by stretching out your neck and lowering your head, so that the lower part of your chin presses against the nearest edge of the glass."

Along the early American frontier, cattle roundup cooks stopped cowboys from hiccuping by cutting off the rind of a lemon wedge and saturating the lemon in bitters—preferably the Angostura bitters (bitters help with digestion, so the cooks carried some in the chuck wagon). The cook added a large dollop of sugar and gave it to the patient to suck. This usually worked very quickly.

Ginger hiccup cures abound throughout the Old World. Here are two old Chinese hiccup remedies. DIRECTIONS: Mix ginger juice with an equal amount of honey. Drink slowly. An alternative is to use fresh ginger slices. Put one ginger slice in the mouth, chew it slowly and swallow the juice. By the time you eat several slices, the hiccups should vanish. The Chinese advise patients with a mouth infection or laryngitis not to use this ginger juice remedy for the hiccups.

In Sweden, villagers once combined breath and movement to cure hiccups. DIRECTIONS: Hold your breath. Join the thumb of each hand with the little finger. Make wide circles with both hands. Evidentally, mental and physical exertion in creating wide circles and the touching of the four finger nerves causes the hiccups to stop.

This old hiccup secret comes from Spain. Unlike the other remedies which involve drinking and tongue and breath, this recommends an indirect approach. DIRECTIONS: Sprinkle one quarter-teaspoon of cayenne pepper powder into half a cup of vinegar. Slowly add small amounts of flour to make a nonrunny paste. Put the paste into a thin cloth and apply it to the diaphragm to stop the hiccup spasms.

In the past, Greeks combined small amounts of coriander, honey, and black pepper to cure hiccups. DIRECTIONS: Combine an eighth-teaspoon of honey, a pinch of powdered coriander, and a pinch of pepper. Put it on the tongue for a minute or so. Wash it off with lukewarm water.

HIGH BLOOD PRESSURE

The heart is a continuously running machine that pumps oxygen-rich blood and nutrients to cells. If there are any mechanical obstacles—deposits of cholesterol lining the arteries, for example—the heart automatically increases its pressure in order to force the blood around the blockages. This automatic increase in pressure causes about sixty million people to develop high blood pressure. Sometimes the pressure also manifests itself in headaches, eye problems, dizziness, even high back pain. A vegetarian diet probably lowers blood pressure because it is low in sodium (salt can elevate pressure) and high in calcium, magnesium, and potassium. Most blood pressure pills deplete body potassium, thus exacerbating the problem they are designed to solve. By eating three servings of potatoes, oranges, or bananas per day, you can lower sodium intake about ten percent and elevate potassium levels.

Since early times, garlic has been a treasured medicinal plant. Research indicates it might work because it dilates the blood vessels, making it easier for the heart to pump blood through the arteries. Garlic also binds toxic minerals and heavy metals such as lead and cadmium and transports them out of the body. DIRECTIONS: Cut slivers of fresh garlic into soups, salads, and meats whenever you can. Try out your own regimen of daily garlic—either with capsules or fresh, crushed garlic in a fruit drink such as pineapple juice. Pineapple and fresh garlic are a successful combination.

Herbalist Sebastian Kneipp describes three Bavarian water treatments for high blood pressure. He advises a water enema, which he feels may reduce internal pressure; hot baths or saunas that induce sweating; and a two-hour clay-water foot wrapping for a high blood pressure headache. DIRECTIONS: For the wrapping, dip a long, three-inch wide cloth (Ace bandages are good) in about four tablespoons of water in which about half a cup of Fuller's earth or neutral clay has been dissolved. Wring out the bandage and wrap the calf of the leg from the ankle to the knee. The wrapping works by temporarily diverting blood from the head and makes the headache disappear. Discontinue application if there are palpitations.

In some parts of the Asian world, people believe that the ear is a microcosm of the entire body. Thus, in Ayurvedic medicine, you can help maintain and lower pressure with ear massage. The ear massage is thought to rebalance the body internally by acting on the energy in the small and large intestine. DIRECTIONS: Start massaging where the ear is attached to the head and continue along the edges of the ear, then to the center area.

The ancient Chinese had a four-pronged approach to normalizing blood pressure and preventing the cholesterol buildup that clogs arteries and contributes to high blood pressure. They advised eating foods that "soften" blood vessels such as fruit, kelp, and mung bean sprouts; eating foods that reduce blood pressure such as celery, banana, persimmon, and hawthorn fruit; replacing all saturated animal fats such as butter with unsaturated corn, peanut, and sesame oil to reduce the level of cholesterol; and *avoiding* foods with high cholesterol levels such as egg yolk, liver, and kidneys.

Celery juice was often used throughout Europe and also by early American settlers to reduce high blood pressure. Directions: Wash a big batch of organic celery. Squeeze out the juice (use juicer or blender). Add some honey to the juice and warm it in a small pan. Divide the portions into two and drink during the day.

The world-renowned Western-trained Japanese physician Dr. Y. Manaka believes certain finger pressure points reduce high blood pressure. Directions: Starting at each front neck "bump" and moving upwards on an angle over the artery to the jawline and the bottom of the ear, massage first the right carotid artery, then the left carotid artery. Then reach backwards and press the side and back of the neck with all five fingers of the hand. The carotid arteries direct blood flow to the brain.

Over the centuries, the Japanese have learned to depend on the ume plum for medical miracles, including that of lowering blood pressure. In some ways, this is a contradiction—with high blood pressure, patients must eliminate salt and pickling from the diet, yet the ume plum is highly salted and pickled. Nevertheless, its healing abilities are cherished by many health-minded Japanese. Directions: Each day, prepare some healing Japanese bancha tea or boiled water. Cool to lukewarm. Cut an ume plum in half. Add one half to the tea and steep. Drink the tea and eat the plum. Both bancha tea and ume plums are available in jars or sealed packages in health food stores and Oriental markets. The Japanese also utilize diets high in brown rice, other fibrous grains, and many unsalted vegetables to further reduce blood pressure.

HOARSENESS

A day or two of silence can sometimes be a blessing. But laryngitis is a disaster at times when you absolutely must talk or sing. If the loss of voice is not a result of a viral or bacterial infection, investigate these unique cures from the past. They are swift and remarkable.

Lemon can be a powerful antiseptic and cleanser for the body. Coupled with honey in hot lemonade, the duo becomes a potent remedy to overcome hoarseness. DIRECTIONS: Wash and scrub three lemons. Squeeze out the juice and discard the seeds. Add the juice and the clean rinds to just-boiled water. Add five tablespoons of honey and mix thoroughly. Bring up again to a high heat. Drink while hot. Repeat as often as needed.

The ancient Romans attributed sixty-one remedies to the anise plant. Among the remedies was the eating of the licorice-like anise seeds to ease hoarseness. DIRECTIONS: Chew a few seeds at a time or drink some Anisette, an anise liqueur. Add bruised anise seeds—or one tablespoon of the liqueur—to any lemon and/or honey-laden hot herbal tea.

Several thousand years ago, Chinese doctors discovered that one of the keys to regaining one's voice was gentle pressure on the center of the tongue. DIRECTIONS: With a clean handkerchief pull the tongue forward, slowly but firmly, in all directions. This relaxes the uvula, the small grape-like soft tissue hanging from the palate above the root of the tongue.

 In the past century, herbalist Sebastian Kneipp taught the entire European continent how to use water, often cold water, to prevent and cure a variety of health problems. One of Kneipp's most remarkable teachings involves cold water compresses for throat problems, a strategy that brilliantly utilizes the body's physiology and reaction to water. The "trick" is to cover the wet compress with a dry wool cloth. Then, because the cold is trapped, the body proceeds to heat the compress from *within*, a process that Kneipp discovered would break up congestions and have a soothing effect on throat or windpipe irritation. Directions: Prepare a clean dish towel, two safety pins, and a woolen or flannel scarf. Fold the dish towel lengthwise into three parts. Dip into cold water and wring it out. Fold the damp, wet compress around the throat and pin it securely with the safety pin. Immediately cover the wet compress with a larger wool scarf and pin it. Allow no air to penetrate to the wet compress! (Some people may like to cover the cold compress with some brown paper or plastic to doubly seal it.) The body marshals internal heat within minutes, and the compress should start to get really warm in about ten to fifteen minutes. If it doesn't, the body's reaction is too weak, or the compress isn't sealed. In that case, immediately discard the wet compress and wear a cotton or wool turtleneck sweater instead. This isn't as effective, but it heats the throat area.

From Spain we find this soothing speaker's gargle for noninfectious laryngitis. Directions: Combine one and a half cups of barley malt (any good ale or beer can work), and enough rosewater and honey to fill a half pint bottle. Thoroughly dissolve the honey. Gargle as often as needed. Drugstores and health food stores carry rosewater.

In the nineteenth century, Dr. William Fitzgerald discovered that continued pressure on the wisdom teeth could help singers and speakers. Dr. Fitzgerald describes a singer who had suffered a progressive loss of hearing and who could no longer sing on pitch. Acting on a hunch, Fitzgerald gave her a rubber eraser to tuck between her top and bottom wisdom teeth and bite on *hard,* several times a day, especially before singing or rehearsing. Within only a few weeks of this therapy, the singer completely recovered her recent hearing loss and regained her ability to sing on pitch.

The old reliable *Theatrum Botanium* recommends lavender as a cure for hoarseness. DIRECTIONS: "Two spoonfuls of the distilled water of the flowers taken, doth helpe those that have lost their speech or voyce, restoring it them again." Check your local health food store for distilled lavender water. Follow package directions.

European immigrants to this country were often without doctors to minister to them. From the Native Americans, they learned the value of slippery elm for hoarseness and sore throat. The herb made from the bark of the tree becomes sticky and mucilaginous when it is mixed with water and is easily formed into lozenges. DIRECTIONS: Excellent slippery elm lozenges are available in health food stores. Follow package directions.

INCONTINENCE

Our internal bladder muscles can sag as we grow older. This occasionally causes minor leakage embarrassments during laughing or coughing. Other urinary incontinence situations can also develop with severe constipation, a prostatic enlargement, or delivery problems during childbirth. Now and then drugs used for other ailments cause incontinence as a side effect.

The Chinese worked out two emergency points to temporarily control the urgent need to urinate. Pressure on these points only works for about half an hour at a time, but even this can be useful at times. DIRECTIONS: Press deeply on the outside edge of the right foot, just behind the bony prominence below the small toe. Then, press deeply on the outside of the right foot in line with the little toe, midway between the toe and the ankle.

To control incontinence, Bavarians used a technique called cold water treading. Cold water treading is also useful as a wakeup treatment and, amazingly, also relaxes the body before sleep. Do not allow feeble invalids, people with heart or circulation problems, or any child under four years of age to use this treatment. DIRECTIONS: The goal is eventually to be able to walk in a few inches of cold water in the tub. Start the therapy by putting one big toe, then another under cold running water for a few seconds. In a short time, the cold should feel good. Increase the amount of time the feet and ankles are under the cold running water each time you do this. Graduate to walking in cold water up to your calves. Hold on to a guard rail and walk in place for a few minutes.

A woman in Camden Town, London, had a huge old trunk in her outer hallway which was filled with clothing and books from a great-great uncle and aunt who had once lived in India. Among the treasures, the trunk contained two very old hand-written receipt books. One flourishing entry read: "WATER—Too Much," followed by a midwife's directions for the great-great aunt to prevent incontinence. DIRECTIONS: "Midwife G. says: For The Involuntary Dripping Of Water—work to make the bladder muscles stronger. 1. When voiding [urinating], tense the muscles to temporarily control the flow. 2. Before or during bowel movement, contract the muscles as if to hold back a movement. 3. Squeeze the vaginal muscles. 4. Squeeze the lower buttocks muscles to contract the genital area. Do each exercise every day, several times a day until problem of dripping is solved."

Traditional Japanese shiatsu also has a suggestion for incontinence. DIRECTIONS: For involuntary dripping of urine, Japanese practitioners recommended massage and deep pressure on the back, especially over the buttock area. They also searched for any painful spots on the back, then pressed them several times each day.

Ohashi, a modern shiatsu master, speaks of his early memories in Japan, when his father continually shamed him about his bedwetting. "It seemed the more I tried to stop, the more nervous I became and the more I wet the bed," Ohashi says. His mother cured him with general *shiatsu* massage. DIRECTIONS: These are Ohashi's instructions: Place the child on his back. Stretch and open both his legs. Pinch each of his toes with your thumb and index finger and then pull them gently. Massage each toe for two to three minutes. Pinch his big toe with your thumb and index finger; still holding the toe, raise his leg until the toe is two inches away from the child's head. Shake the leg by the toe. Repeat this with each toe.

The oil made from the flowers of St. John's Wort (*Hypericum perforatum*) is an ancient European remedy for incontinence. But be careful, exposure to sunlight after taking the oil internally may cause a dermatitis in some. DIRECTIONS: Place five drops of St. John's Wort in an ounce of cold water and stir. Drink four times a day.

For many centuries, the Chinese have employed mui plus water for nighttime incontinence. Mui is cranberry (*Vaccinitium macrocarpon*). DIRECTIONS: In a blender, combine one package of unsugared frozen cranberries with several cups of pure water. Chinese patients drink four ounces of the juice at four o'clock each day. Organic cranberry juice without added sugar is available in health food stores or through the mail.

INFECTIONS

Infective agents from microorganisms assail us constantly. Most of the time our immune systems can fight the critters off. But despite the availability and importance of modern antibiotics, it is worthwhile to learn these practical and safe remedies from our useful past. Don't let these substitute for your physician's advice, however.

The Egyptians used honey in five hundred of their nine hundred known medicinal remedies. Why? Dr. Guido Majno of Harvard University Medical School conducted laboratory tests and discovered that honey acts as a natural antibiotic. Part of the honey breaks down to H_2O_2, hydrogen peroxide, the common household disinfectant. DIRECTIONS: Dab on honey to heal sores and small cuts. Honey also attracts fluid, and when fluid is drawn from a wound, the bacteria are killed. This is the reason the Russians often put *sugar* on a wound. Sugar also draws out fluid.

Rosemary first flourished in the Mediterranean area, and, over the centuries, it evolved as a powerful tonic and stimulant. A *Lytell Herball* published in 1550 recommends rosemary for infections. (Also see "Vinegar Of The Four Thieves" below.) "Take the flower of rosemary and put them in a lynen clothe, and so boyle them in fayre cleane water to the halfe and cole (cool) it, and drynke it for it is much worthe against all evyls in the body."

During the 1300s, nearly half the population of Europe was killed by a terrifying epidemic of the "bubonic plague" or Black Death—so named because dying patients turned black. This plague is spread by the bite of a flea from an infected rodent and is passed through the air from person to person by coughing. Fortunately, we can now overcome plague with modern antibiotics. But the following remedy, the "Vinegar of the Four Thieves," developed during the Black Death, has a fascinating history. As the legend goes, four thieves were caught robbing homes of dying plague victims and hauled into court. The magistrate looked at the thieves with disbelief mixed with awe. "Everyone who has direct contact with this plague catches it. How did you four survive?" he asked. The thieves claimed they had a *secret* plague-preventive remedy and bartered their freedom for the recipe. This anti-infection remedy was popular for several centuries and was noted in the 1856 "Receipt Book Of A Virginia Housewife." DIRECTIONS: "Take lavender, rosemary, sage, wormwood, rue and mint of each a large handful, put into a pot of earthenware, pour on them four quarts of very strong vinegar, cover the pot closely, and put a board on the top. Keep in the hottest sun two weeks, then strain and bottle it, putting in each bottle a clove of garlic. When it has settled in the bottle and become clear, pour if off gently; do this until you get it all free from sediment. The proper time to make it is when the herbs are in full vigor, in June. This vinegar is very refreshing in crowded rooms, in the apartment of the sick, and is peculiarly grateful when sprinkled about the house in damp weather."

In Chechnyna in the Caucasus mountains, they have an old tradition of curing an abscess by applying well-chewed, salted bread to the abscess. The Chechens, who are the largest of the North Caucasian nationalities in the present-day Russian federation, say this is the way their old village healers avoided amputation, even in gangrenous cases. While chewed bread might sound strange to modern ears, an unexpected validation has turned up from American researchers who have discovered the human tongue contains an invisible, heretofore-unknown antibiotic shield that can be transferred to food by chewing. Directions: Cut a large slice of freshly-baked whole wheat or rye bread. Sprinkle it with salt (some Chechens add melted butter, too). Chew the salted bread thoroughly. Apply to the abscess and attach with a gauze bandage. Change bread and bandage twice a day.

One of the early advocates of super-hygiene for doctors, nurses, and patients was Elizabeth Blackwell, born in 1821, the first woman doctor in the United States. After overcoming great obstacles, she was finally recognized by male doctors because of her superb medical leadership during the Civil War. She opened her own hospital and was in the forefront of the fight for super-cleanliness in hospitals to avoid passing on infection. Directions: At all times, but especially during a household illness, use lots of hot water and soap to scrub hands and kitchen utensils. Scrub chopping blocks carefully and add clorox to laundry items. Avoid salmonella contamination from chicken and hamburger by carefully washing hands and area of contact with the meat. Carefully wash all fresh fruits and vegetables.

Burdock root and leaves (*Arctium lappa*) have been an invaluable plant medicine since medieval times. The root and/or leaves were generally used to "purify" the blood and rebalance the body during an illness. Here are two European folk remedies. DIRECTIONS: First, when an infection from sores or wounds swells the arms or the legs, apply washed and slightly cooked burdock leaves to infected sores, bruises, and skin inflammations. To cleanse the system, especially when there's an abscess or pus anywhere on the body, boil several ounces of clean, dried burdock root in one quart of water for twenty minutes. Strain out the root. Heat up this tea, add honey, and drink one cupful one hour before each meal. Continue until the infection is resolved.

During any infection, the Egyptians, Romans, Greeks, and others after them, ate enormous quantities of garlic. Fresh garlic cloves act like gigantic antibiotic scrubbing brushes, cleansing the body of bacterial invaders. DIRECTIONS: Add garlic to soups, stews, poultry, salads—anywhere you can.

INFLAMMATION

The word inflammation originates from "flammare," which means "to set on fire" in Latin. The swelling, heat, pain, and redness is the body's defensive reaction to either bacterial invasion or trauma. Inflammation can occur in any tissue or organ of the body. Ancient prescriptions describe remedies for dozens of inflammations ranging from the skin to the joints, glands, and other body areas.

As the last-century Germans experimented with water as a medical modality, they discovered the value of hot and cold remedies. DIRECTIONS: If a joint is hot or swollen, do not apply heat, but apply a cold pack or soft ice bag. Use for twenty minutes at a time and repeat as needed. If the joint is inflamed but not hot, many people prefer wet heat (compresses, poultices, hot water bottles) to sooth the pain. In that case, alternate ice and moist heat.

Gentian (*Gentiana*) takes its name from a king of Illyria who initially discovered its ability to reduce fevers. In medieval times, gentian was the most important ingredient in a famous secret cure-all preparation. DIRECTIONS: Through the centuries, the French and Germans employed a tincture of gentian to alleviate gall bladder inflammation. For each tablespoon of water, add three drops of gentian tincture. Sip three times a day. Gentian tincture is available through health food stores and mail order.

Castor oil poultices are very soothing for inflammations of the joints. DIRECTIONS: Dip a soft flannel cloth into a deodorized castor oil. Wring it out and wrap it around the affected joint. Cover with a piece of plastic and wrap everything together with an Ace bandage, obtainable from a drugstore. Velcro straps are also useful for poultices, ice packs, and compresses. They are more difficult to obtain. Try ordering them through drugstores specializing in injury and rehabilitation aids.

The pineapple plant, which is, of course, neither a pine nor an apple, originated in the West Indies and in South America. It contains bromelain, an enzyme that has anti-inflammatory abilities. DIRECTIONS: The West Indian islanders eat the yellow pulp of the pineapple to lessen internal inflammation and also apply it topically on a variety of skin inflammations.

There is much wisdom in the practical food and spices eaten throughout the world. In India, they use turmeric (*Curcuma longa*) mainly to give curry its color. But turmeric also has several medicinal abilities—it can divert sinus and joint inflammations. In Ayurvedic medicine, turmeric is also added to salt for a daily nasal wash to prevent sinusitis. Directions: Use turmeric as a spice in food or take capsules or tablets available in health food stores. Use an Ayurvedic narial nasal cup filled with lukewarm water and a quarter-teaspoon coarse salt. Use this spouted cup to allow the fluid to flow in, through, and out the other nostril while breathing through the mouth. An alternative is to pinch a "spout" into the rim of a paper cup.

Thyme and its oil, both of which are thought to bring congested blood to the surface, were commonly used in Asia Minor as a topical application to relieve joint inflammation. Directions: Drop a quarter-teaspoon of thyme oil into water. Dip in a cloth, wring it out, and apply repeatedly to areas of sciatic or arthritic inflammation.

Peppermint tea is an old reliable European treatment to cool inflamed joints. The menthol it contains has a special cooling and invigorating effect on the skin. Directions: Add a pot of peppermint tea to bathwater, or soak a cloth in peppermint tea and apply to an inflamed joint.

For urinary or joint inflammation, British healers and herbalists prescribed celery juice drinks made from the whole plant. Directions: Toss a few stalks of celery in a food processor or juicer, liquify, and flavor with any culinary spice such as cinnamon or nutmeg to taste. Drink as inclined.

Red clover (*Trifolium pratense*) was first introduced into America in the seventeenth century from England and was marketed by various Shaker communities as an excellent health remedy. For lymphatic swellings, early American herbalists processed red clover into a topical ointment. DIRECTIONS: Cover the fresh flowers with water and simmer over low heat or in a slow cooker for two days. Strain. Heat again so that most of the water evaporates. Combine the residue with an equal amount of ointment such as pure lanolin or Vaseline and apply to the swelling of inflammation.

Marshmallow (*Althaea offininalis*) comes from the Greek word "althaea" which means to heal. The plant expands in water and provides a soft, mucilaginous product that has been used since ancient Egyptian times to heal internal and external inflammations. DIRECTIONS: The first century botanical observer Pliny praised it highly and tells us what to do: "Whoever swallows daily half a cupful of the juice of any of the mallows will be immune to all disease."

The Swiss regularly used calendula (or pot marigold) ointment on any skin inflammation, especially dry skin, dry eczema, or sore nipples. DIRECTIONS: A wide variety of calendula products are available in health food stores. Follow package directions.

Strawberries are cooling to the skin and can reduce sunburn or other inflammations. DIRECTIONS:

Apply crushed berries directly on burned or inflamed skin. Rinse off after a few moments.

Oil of cinnamon has had an entrancing aroma and a powerful reputation as a germicide down through the centuries. Hippocrates says, "If there is inflammation and pain in the womb take rose leaves, cinnamon, cassia. . . fumigate therewith and it will sooth the pain."

Witch hazel extract, a Native American discovery, reduces sudden skin inflammations and swellings like magic. Sometimes Native Americans combined witch hazel with blueberries to heal skin inflammations. DIRECTIONS: Mash equal amounts of Dickinson witch hazel and blueberries together, then apply to skin. Rinse off later.

Licorice comes from the Mediterranean and has been used since 500 B.C. to relieve inflammation, especially gastric inflammation. In Chinese medicine, herbalists use licorice to "detoxify" the body. DIRECTIONS: To make a tonic wine of licorice, steep a piece of the root in gin or vodka for a few weeks. Strain out the root. Drink in small doses after meals. Avoid licorice if you have a rapid heartbeat or high blood pressure. Capsules and tablets of deglycyrrhized licorice are also available.

INFLUENZA (ALSO SEE COLDS)

The flu is an acute viral infection involving the respiratory tract. It occurs in isolated cases, in epidemics, or in "pandemics"—epidemics that simultaneously occur on many continents. The pandemic of 1918-1919 killed twenty-one million people throughout the world. The best way to defend against the flu is to beef up the immune system and to use natural methods to cut the illness short. Here's how our ancient ancestors survived the flu.

Mustard seed powder has a powerful external action on the body. Technically it is a rubefacient, a substance that brings blood to the surface of the skin. Such substances switch the body from a static state of ill health into an active healing state. The Siberians have a strong affinity for mustard powder treatments. People who feel on the verge of flu in Siberia fill their socks with powdered mustard and walk in the mustard-filled socks for three days to halt the attack. Directions: If you have callused feet that can withstand the slight burning sensation of mustard, follow the Siberian method. Or if your feet are a little more delicate, run a few inches of hot water in the bathtub and dissolve two or three tablespoons of powdered mustard in the water. Immerse ankles in the hot water for a five minute footbath. The footbath draws congestion away from the chest and nasal passages and thoroughly stimulates the body. It's best to take this footbath just before a nap or before going to sleep. Mustard powder is an everyday spice shelf item in supermarkets.

Throughout the world, people drink a great deal of water to flush flu germs that have been killed by the immune system out of the body. Lemonade and red raspberry tea also help to reduce fever.

Each day to ward off illness, especially colds and flu, many Japanese adhere to an old tradition and eat a pickled, salted umeboshi plum. Although some find "umes" too salty for their taste, many healthy adults swear by these health-restoring fruits. DIRECTIONS: Advocates of this tradition believe that eating the roasted plum can halt any illness in its tracks. Some advocates also make a strong Japanese tea called bancha and steep the roasted plum in the tea. They drink the tea and eat the plum. Try either of these methods. Umeboshi plums are available in oriental grocery stores and in many health food stores in sealed packages and jars.

One homeopath asked a riddle: Why is the flu both positive and negative? The answer: "Sometimes the eyes have it, sometimes the nose." Quips aside, everyone should explore this one-hundred-fifty-year-old system of healing. Homeopathy is avidly prescribed by European doctors, especially those in Germany, France, and Great Britain. Its value is especially well-demonstrated in its ability to abort, control, or shorten an influenza attack. In Great Britain, they are justifiably proud that no homeopath lost a patient in the world-wide pandemic of 1918. DIRECTIONS: While there are many single homeopathic remedies for the flu, it is often more effective to use an over-the-counter *combination* remedy such as "Oscillicoccinum." People who use this remedy praise its ability to keep flu attacks at bay. The secret is to use it the moment you feel slightly indisposed. The later you take it, the less effective it will be. You can find Oscillicoccinum in health food stores.

INSECT BITES

Summer weather brings out lush vegetation, tennis players, and, unfortunately, people-biting insects. The bites of some insects are tolerable, but others are painful and even, occasionally, toxic or infectious. Our ancient ancestors discovered simple and safe aromas and remedies to repel insects and to heal, soothe, and desensitize insect bites.

Plant medicine often offers interesting paradoxes. Lavender has a beguiling and fresh aroma to humans, but bugs hate the smell! We still follow the old tradition of adding sprigs of lavender to stored linens, wools, and blankets. The rural people of England wore lavender "necklaces" to repel bugs. Directions: Dip the fringe of a cotton scarf or a piece of absorbent cotton in lavender oil, drain it, and hang it around the neck as an informal necklace or scarf. It prevents bugs from attacking that part of the body.

Nature offers still another contradiction with amiable lemon balm. The Greeks observed that lemon balm was a magnet for honey bees. But oddly, when applied on humans, the essential oil squeezed from the leaves of this same lemon balm, repels bees as well as other insects. Directions: Apply the essential oil directly on the skin to repel bees or to relieve the pain of insect stings.

When the first domesticated horse was brought from Asia to Egypt and Arabia in 2000 B.C., his importers also brought along native oats to feed the animal. Later, oats became a major crop in Ancient Greece and Rome and, afterwards, a significant source of food for people in such cold climates as Iceland, Norway, Sweden, Ireland, and Scotland. What's more, oats soon became an important internal and topical healer in these cold countries as well. Among its many uses, village healers found that a wet mash of oats healed the pain of insect bites. Directions: Apply slightly wet Aveeno, a commercial suspended-particle oat bath preparation, to the bite or add between a half to a full cup of blended powdered oats to bathwater. Such applications instantly overcome pain and inflammation from rashes and bites. Aveeno is available from health food stores.

Aromatic basil (*Ocimum basilicum*) leaves are one of America's favorite additions to pasta. In Arab countries, where the basil scent is especially prized, the leaves are used as an aphrodisiac to be worn by men when visiting women, as a deodorant, a headache aid, and an insect bite remedy. DIRECTIONS: Bruise a fresh leaf and rub it on insect bites to reduce itching and inflammation.

Throughout the world, ancient people applied mud poultices to instantly relieve the pain of an insect bite. DIRECTIONS: Mix earth and water together when outdoors and dab on any bite. Keep neutral clay, an invaluable asset for many first aid applications, in an accessible jar for indoor applications.

The large flat leaves of the lowly wayside plant, plantain (*Plantago major*), give instant relief when applied to bites and stings. Plantain has been used by gypsies throughout the world and by Native Americans who sold it to settlers as a cure-all ointment. Ancient Anglo-Saxons called the plant "waybread" and applied the leaves to bee stings and slow-healing wounds. The plant is a common weed found in parks and by every wayside. DIRECTIONS: Tear off an *unsprayed* leaf, bruise it slightly, and apply to bite, sting, or bruise.

Three ancient martial arts trigger points help control the pain of insect bites. Two are on the outside of each foot directly below the little toe. DIRECTIONS: For an insect bite that produces a hot, red skin, press the *Chou Kou* point every five minutes. This point is immediately under the end of the smallest toe below the first bony protuberance. If bitten by a spider, bee, or wasp, press the *Tsing-Kou* point. It is slightly below the *Chou Kou* point, midway between the toes and the ankle in line with the little toe. If the skin is cold, also press the *Ledum* point on the left side of the chest, between the second and third ribs from the top, about midway between the nipple and the breastbone.

All over the world, onions have been used for all kinds of health problems. Traditionally, the Amish people applied a freshly cut onion to relieve the pain of insect bites and stings. DIRECTIONS: Slice a piece of onion and apply it to the injured skin until it stops hurting.

In most Asian countries, people overcome the itching and inflammation of insect bites with a poultice of damp green tea leaves. DIRECTIONS: Mix one teaspoon green tea leaves with four tablespoons of water. Allow the mixture to sit until all the water is absorbed. Then apply the mash of damp tea leaves on the insect bite.

INSOMNIA

Despite impressive laboratory research, we humans continue to be beset by the same sleep problems as those who lived in antiquity. Fortunately, our ancestor's answers are surprisingly effective.

Sleepless people in China were told to repeatedly yawn deeply just before going to bed. When in bed, they were advised to place the tip of the tongue behind the lower teeth and to concentrate on holding the tongue there until they fell asleep. It prevented them from thinking about their problems so they could relax and sleep.

When Alexander the Great conquered Egypt, his soldiers learned some basic Egyptian medicine, including the belief that eating garlic promoted sleep. The Greeks brought these Egyptian ideas back to their native country. DIRECTIONS: Just before going to bed, mash one or two cloves of garlic, then add a few drops of olive oil. Slather this on some hearty bread and eat. To eliminate the strong odor of raw garlic, chew fennel seeds or parsley. Red onion was also used in this way throughout Europe.

The ancient Brits, as well as other Europeans, knew that most parts of the aromatic hops plant could produce a tea that deeply encouraged sleep. DIRECTIONS: In past centuries, the hops were simply sewed into a sleep-coaxing pillow. Such pillows are available today in shops that specialize in herbs. Occasionally, restore the strength of the pillow by putting it in the sun.

Early American pioneers discovered that the beautiful red clover flower was a treasure of an herb. The tea tasted good, calmed the body, and was a useful sleep remedy. DIRECTIONS: To make red clover tea, add boiling water to two tablespoons of fresh or dried flowers, steep, and strain out the flowers. Add a drop of honey. Honey, the ambrosia from the bees, was also used throughout the ancient world as a prime sleep aid. Because it helps the body retain liquid, it fosters sleep by helping to overcome the need to get up to urinate.

Cold water can be applied in different ways to contribute to adequate sleep. The following are two favorite German remedies. DIRECTIONS: Briefly run cold water over the ankles just before going to bed. Or take a brief, cold sitz bath. Run a few inches of cold water in the bath, then sit in it immersing only the lower extremities. Eventually you can increase the time span from a mere moment to a few minutes. These remedies enhance sleep and strengthen and harden the body against illness. Older folks with circulation or heart trouble should not sit in shallow, cold baths.

The ancient Chinese believed that the body's sleep control center is just under the nail of the big toe, on the corner of the side closest to the other toes. DIRECTIONS: Just before sleep, press this point. The Japanese found it helpful to massage the soles of the feet, as well, several hours before bedtime.

IRREGULAR PERIODS

From Hippocrates' time onward, doctors throughout the world prescribed plants to adjust irregular menstrual periods. Eleanor of Aquitaine, born in 1122, accompanied her first husband King Louis of France on the Second Crusade. Her first-aid kit included many of the commonly-known plants that affected the menstrual cycle. In later centuries, homeopathic remedies emerged for many health situations, including those of heavy bleeding, bloating, and delayed periods. Keep in mind that anything that brings on a period can cause a miscarriage if you're pregnant and be sure to consult first with your doctor.

During the last century and a half, many European women found the homeopathic Magnesia phos. was an easy remedy for simple menstrual cramps.

When there was no pathological cause for bleeding, ancient French herbalists prescribed the calendula (*Calendula offininalis*) plant for treatment of irregular periods, as an antidote to profuse periods, prolonged periods, or periods that produced excessive clots. DIRECTIONS: To make the tea, women either added the flowers to boiling water or added sixteen drops of calendula tincture to a cup of boiling water. In addition, to alleviate menstrual problems of any sort, they applied a hot mash of cooked calendula flowers to the pelvic and lower back area.

When Eleanor of Aquitaine was divorced by King Louis of France, she found another love in Henry Plantagenet, soon to become the king of England. As the queen of England, she soon observed the English admiration for "mother thyme," so called because of its use in uterine disorders. Thyme was cherished for its ability to control heavy menstrual flow. DIRECTIONS: Make thyme tea with a tablespoon of dried leaves and steep in cup of boiled water. Strain out leaves. Those on the threshold of pregnancy should avoid thyme since it is a uterine stimulant.

Even in the earliest centuries, women applied hot herbs encased in cloths to help with menstrual cramps. In the last centuries we have rubber hot water bottles. DIRECTIONS: Apply the bottle to the abdomen or to the lower back. Heat feels necessary and extremely comfortable when one has cramps, but it can also stimulate additional bleeding.

Early Anglo Saxons valued the use of agrimony for heavy bleeding and wounds. By the fifteenth century, they had even devised Arquebusade Water, a renowned battlefield remedy containing agrimony and other astringent herbs that could stop bleeding. Women of the area often drank a mild tea of agrimony root to control excessive menstrual bleeding.

Basil (*Ocimum basilicum*) was a beloved staple of early Greek gardens. The first-century observer Pliny wrote that this aromatic plant was steeped in rosewater (or oil) and vinegar to create an antifatigue liniment which was also often used during menstrual periods. For menstrual unease, the liniment was applied to the lower back and pelvic areas. In England, women drank *fresh* basil tea to precipitate menstruation. DIRECTIONS: For tea, use one tablespoon of dried or fresh leaves to one cup of boiling water. Steep for five to ten minutes. Strain. To make the liniment, steep a handful of fresh or dried basil leaves in a cup of rosewater and a cup of apple cider vinegar. Stand two weeks in a warm place. Strain out herbs. Apply as liniment.

For delayed menstruation, each day before meals, women of the Caribbean islands drink warm ginger tea or eat a nut-sized piece of ginger root. European women learned about the value of ginger from islanders. DIRECTIONS: To overcome painful cramps and nausea, place several drops of the essential oil of ginger on a sugar cube and either eat the sugar or drop it in a cup of calendula, peppermint, or chamomile tea.

For painful periods and as a general tonic and soother of menstrual headaches, women of Germany, France, and Holland drank peppermint tea.

Throughout history, fennel seeds have provided relief for digestive problems. German women discovered the seeds could alleviate excessive menstrual pain. To this day, American descendants of German settlers use fennel in this way. DIRECTIONS: Steep a handful of fennel seeds in cup of boiling water, strain out the seeds, and drink the tea during difficult periods.

Carrots are a tonic food rich in vitamins and minerals, soothing and curative for any number of health problems, including menstrual irregularity. Initially European herbalists applied the grated vegetable only as a poultice to heal sties, old sores, swellings, and tumors. But Swedish settlers to America soon discovered an entirely new use for carrots: to control menstrual pain. DIRECTIONS: Add a daily dose of grated carrots to the diet.

Many plants, including hawthorn, are astringent and will cut down on bleeding. In Belgium and Holland, women drank hawthorn berry tea to reduce heavy bleeding. DIRECTIONS: Add a handful of hawthorn berries to a pot of boiling water. Steep five minutes, then strain and drink.

The seeds of fenugreek, one of the oldest medical herbs in the world, were served by the ancient Egyptians as a warming tea to ease menstrual pain. Avoid if considering pregnancy—fenugreek is a uterine stimulant.

Lemon Balm (*Melissa offininalis*) is an herb favored since the Middle Ages as an elixir to overcome almost any uterine problem. European healers made up potions of *Melissa* to overcome infertility, soothe pain during a period, and stimulate a delayed period.

The medicinal value of chamomile is concentrated in the yellow centers of the flowers. The double variety which was introduced to the rest of Europe from Spain in the Middle Ages, was well-established as a medicine by the sixteenth century. In France, Spain, and Germany, the apple-smelling chamomile flower was employed as a tea and as a poultice for menstrual disorders. Chamomile tea is still one of the first choices for women interested in reestablishing a more regular pattern of menstruation. Directions: For menstrual pain, apply a hot poultice of the flowers to the groin and lower back.

Garcia Da Orta, in his *The Simples and Drugs of India*, says the fruit of the mango was used as medicine since the fifteenth century and, in an early stage of growth, is styptic in its actions. Three centuries later, homeopaths experimented with mango and rediscovered its ability to stop bleeding. They utilized tiny, much-diluted pills containing early growth mango for passive hemorrhages, including uterine bleeding.

MEMORY LOSS

Even people with terrific memories sometimes temporarily lose a name or a fact—and the odd thing is, that name and fact can leap out seconds later. Scientists don't actually know how memory works except that immediate, short-term, and long-term memories each require the use of at least some of the brain's two million neurons. Here are some wonderful natural aids from thc past that can help a wilting memory.

 The childhood tongue twister, "Peter Piper picked a peck of pickled peppers" referred to cayenne pepper (*Capsicum annuum*), named by the Greeks, "I bite." Cayenne was originally used as a powdered spice to make bland food more palatable. Gradually over the centuries, and remarkably all through Indian and African tribes as well as in Europe and the Americas, it achieved note as a medicine, too. It was known for its restorative and stimulating abilities in illness, sluggish digestion, even flatulence. English herbalists also recommended the herb to improve memory and believed the pepper could help deter senility. Directions: Sprinkle cayenne powder on food or add it in tiny amounts to herbal teas such as peppermint, sage, rosemary, fennel, or lemon balm.

Sage (*Salvia offininalis*) has appeared throughout history as a stimulant and an aid to health. In medieval times, purple sage was a traditional ingredient of memory and longevity tonics, one that could be depended on to center one's energy. Directions: Boil a cup of water and add one pinch of sage. Strain and drink one cup a day. You can also add rosemary, another traditional memory aid.

Ginseng root powder has an important place in preserving memory through Asian culture. Directions: Use a pinch of ginseng powder in some tea to enhance memory. While many people use ginseng every day, it is a powerful herbal alternative that should be used only when you need it.

To maintain and improve memory, the Amish use a hazelnut therapy. Directions: Eat hazelnuts for nine days. Start with six nuts then add an extra nut each day. This can be repeated several times a year.

It is widely known that elephants have excellent memories. In India, those who worked with the elephants noticed that the animals fed extensively on the herb gotu kola. This may have been the reason ancient Ayurvedic practitioners employed gotu kola (*Centella asiatica*) as a nerve tonic to promote mental calm and clarity. Traditional Appalachian herbalists also use this herb "for the brain." Today, holistic physicians sometimes prescribe gotu kola to enhance circulation throughout the body. They generally suggest standardized capsules such as Cellu-Var, made by Enzymatic Therapy, which contains gotu kola and two other herbs: butcher's broom (*Ruscus aculeatus*) and horse chestnut (*Aesculus hippocustanum*).

Along both the European and African shores of the Mediterranean, fennel is both a prized vegetable and a classic medicinal remedy. In Algeria and Tunisia, the leaves of fennel are made into a strong tea and used as a general brain tonic and memory stimulant. In the mountains of Bavaria, the renowned herbalist Sebastian Kneipp also recommended fennel tea, and fennel baths, especially to rid the body of impurities. DIRECTIONS: Eat the whole fennel plant, especially the leaves. Make a tea of fresh or dried fennel leaves using two tablespoons of bruised leaves to one cup of boiling water. Take baths in strong fennel tea made from leaves or fennel seeds.

Kale is a somewhat ignored, inexpensive "soul" food in America. But in ancient Greece, it was a favorite vegetable that was used to help rheumatism, eyesight, and memory. The plant contains potassium, phosphorus, calcium, and sulphur. DIRECTIONS: Kale can be used in three ways—raw in a salad, cooked as a vegetable, or as a tea. For tea, mince a handful of the leaves, add red pepper and salt to taste, and drop into two cups of boiling water. Steep, cool, and drink strained as a liquid before meals.

Sweet violet (*Viola odorata*) has a wonderful perfume and has often been the first gift between friends and lovers. But the French, who have admired violets for their medicinal value, also used them to restore a weak memory. One renowned French actress had a bouquet of violets sent to her dressing room before each performance for thirty years. Legend has it that this beautiful actress stripped the petals of the fresh violets to make tea. Violets to remember her lines? DIRECTIONS: Eat the raw leaves each day in a salad, or make a strong tea with the leaves and the flowers using two tablespoons of violets to one cup of boiling water. Steep, strain, and drink.

Ginkgo biloba is one of the oldest medical plants. In ancient Chinese medicine, they used it to stimulate a flagging memory. For the last fifteen years, European scientists have been investigating the effect of ginkgo on memory loss and other common disorders. They discovered that ginkgo improves blood flow to the brain and thus enhances short term memory and alertness. This newly "rediscovered" herb also works with other problems such as atherosclerosis, ringing of the ears, vertigo, and impotence. DIRECTIONS: *Ginkgo biloba* capsules are available in health food stores. Follow package directions.

MUSCLE SPASMS/ CRAMPS

Who hasn't had some sort of muscle spasm in the middle of the night? In general, muscle cramps are painful and usually happen at inconvenient and inappropriate times. Spasms and cramps can occur in any muscle, but usually occur in the calf or foot, frequently while either lying in bed or participating in some sport.

Ever since the original Olympic Games in Greece, athletes were advised to drink copious amounts of water to correct fluid loss from excess sweating to avoid cramps. DIRECTIONS: Drink lots of water before doing any physical activity that might cause sweating. Maintaining fluid may help prevent cramps.

The most instinctive way to deal with a muscle cramp of the toes or leg is to massage the cramped area with your hands. But oddly, this may increase the pain. Ancient Roman soldiers were taught to relieve such cramps by putting weight on the foot. DIRECTIONS: While standing, bend your knees and press your feet downwards, hard against the floor. Stamp the foot or leg that hurts until the cramp eases. For toe cramps during the night, get out of bed as quickly as possible and stand on the ball of the foot with the cramp, rising on your toes. French Foreign Legion soldiers were taught the best way to overcome a nighttime foot cramp was to pull their toes toward their knees.

Over a century and a half ago, Austrians discovered they could relax a muscle cramp by applying an ice pack on the area that hurt. DIRECTIONS: Keep ice packs ready in the freezer. If none are available during an emergency, apply a frozen package of vegetables.

One of Napoleon's generals had unique instructions for preventing muscle cramps. Infantry soldiers were told to take off their shoes and place their legs against the wall or tree for five minutes. DIRECTIONS: To duplicate this old procedure, take off your shoes, lie on the floor, and put your feet on the wall or against the back of a chair or couch. This immediately changes the flow of gravity and creates new patterns of circulation.

There are two Chinese jujitsu and judo points for muscle cramps and spasms on the top of the foot below the separation point of the big toe and next toe. DIRECTIONS: To relieve cramps or spasms, press the *Sing-Tsienn* point directly below the separation between the biggest and the next toe. Then press the *Trae-Tchrong* point, which is two thumb-widths below the *Sing-Tsienn* point.

Walking tours through the English countryside have been a pastime for centuries. During a strenuous day walking up and down hill and dale, most walkers do this simple exercise several times a day to prevent nighttime cramps. DIRECTIONS: Standing in bare feet with arms stretched sideways at shoulder level, face a wall about a foot away. Slowly lean forward until you feel a slight pull in your calf muscles. Hold for several minutes, then return to your normal stance.

Over three hundred years ago, the famous London doctor Dr. Thomas Willis described restless leg syndrome. He characterized it variously as a numbing or stabbing pain, an electric muscle cramp, or a creepy, crawly sensation deep in the legs. The attacks occur when one is at rest. DIRECTIONS: Dr. Willis suggested that restless leg syndrome might be a reaction to caffeine, and he withdrew his patients from any coffee and tea. He also advocated adding the countryside "walking tour" exercise described above.

NASAL AND SINUS CONGESTION

In modern times, we often neglect our sense of smell until a stuffy nose or an inflamed and congested sinus takes it away. Fortunately, we can learn from ancient medicine how to reduce both congestion and inflammation—leaving us free to enjoy the familiar scents of home.

As anyone who has walked through a Christmas tree exhibit can confirm, the smell of pine trees not only makes you feel good, but it opens up the nasal passages. The Amish use this scent to relieve nasal congestion. DIRECTIONS: Boil one quart of water. Add just a few drops of essence of pine or a handful of bruised pine needles and two tablespoons of apple cider vinegar. Carefully place the boiling water on a well-protected table in a closed room so that you can comfortably breathe in the steam for ten to fifteen minutes. A handful of crushed peppermint leaves can be substituted for the pine needles.

A moist heat massage is used throughout Asia to clear the sinuses, reduce nasal congestion, and decrease pain in the face and head. DIRECTIONS: Assemble the following: a hot washcloth, a piece of ginger, a pinch of brown sugar to keep the ginger from irritating, an eyedropper, facial tissues, a bottle of sesame oil, and a rolled towel to be placed under the neck during the massage. Run a bottle of sesame oil under some hot water or encase it in hot cloths to warm it up. Put it aside and keep it warm. Prepare several hot washcloths and put aside. Roll the neck towel and put it aside. Get the facial tissues ready. Grate enough ginger to render three tablespoons of juice. Toss the ginger itself in the garbage. Dilute the juice with half a teaspoon of water and mix with a pinch of brown sugar. Now put the rolled towel under your neck and lean backwards. Gently pat some warm sesame oil on the skin with clockwise circular motions. Apply facial tissues to the oiled face, covering everything but the nose. Apply another thin dribbling of the warm sesame oil over the layer of tissue. Apply a hot washcloth to the *right side* of the face. Keep on applying more cloths until the oil has been absorbed and the right side seems flushed and red. Switch and repeat massage, oil, and hot washcloth treatment on the left side. Now you are ready to take the eye-dropper, fill it with diluted ginger juice, and squeeze three drops into the right nostril. Gently massage the sinus area below the right eye with circular motions. The nasal and sinus congestion will start to break up. It may even cause some tears. Dribble three drops of ginger juice into the left nostril. Gently massage the left sinus area under the eye. Do not do this massage after eating a large meal or if you are menstruating or pregnant.

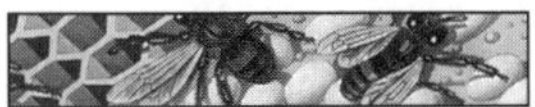 In the past, Russian village healers would convince sinusitis patients to avoid milk because it forms too much mucus.

Massage movements were invented thousands of years ago by Chinese monks to strengthen the sinus area and help alleviate pain from sinus inflammation. DIRECTIONS: Place the tip of the right index finger on the middle of the cheek on level with the nostrils. Gently press downwards. You should feel a little drainage. With the same finger, press and gently squeeze towards the nose. This increases drainage. Repeat on the other side of the face. Hot towels placed on this area will complete the relief.

Yehudi Menuhin, one of the world's greatest violinists, was one of the first people to introduce yoga principles to the United States. Carnegie Hall was filled with enthralled listeners as he demonstrated and explained the significance of yoga postures. Like a master swami, Menuin even cleared his nasal passages with string! Most of us gasped and said we wouldn't and couldn't do that. But then Menuhin told us of the common preventive measures of *daily* washing of the nasal passages with clean, warm water to which a pinch of salt and turmeric (optional) is added. DIRECTIONS: Gently inhale the salt water mixture up one nostril. Tilt your head back and allow the mix to drain into the back of your mouth. Spit out the water. Repeat with the other nostril. The most effective way to enjoy this singular experience is to use an Ayurvedic *neti pot*. This is a small cup with a thin, small spout. The best way to describe it is that it looks like a toy Aladdin's lamp. A handmade porcelain nasal irrigation pot with instructions for use can be obtained by mail order. (See Appendix I.)

Arab nomads use leafy sprays of the exquisite yellow-flowered elecampane (*Inula viscosa*) in a steam bath to clear the head of sinus aches and pains caused by nasal congestion. This herb is also favored for vapor baths designed to reduce stiffness and/or rheumatic pain. DIRECTIONS: Place a handful of elecampane in a non-aluminum pan. Add several cups of boiling water to create steam. Lean over the pan, drape a towel over your head, and allow it to hang down on either side of the bowl. Breathe deeply and allow the steam to liquify the accumulated mucus which may be causing a sinus headache. Be careful not to burn your face.

"Open Sesame!" A mere whiff of that ancient secret Chinese ointment, Tiger Balm, will open clogged nasal passages. The herbs in the balm are healing and will bring blood to the surface of the skin. DIRECTIONS: Apply a tiny, thin coat of Tiger Balm over the sinuses and along the outer edge of the nose. Tiger Balm is available in health food stores.

One of the exceptional healing secrets handed down to us through centuries of use in Asia reveals how parts of the body are connected, and the way you can "reach" and heal an area by pressing on a far-away spot. That is why deep pressure on the joints of the fingers is so effective and often seems almost magical. DIRECTIONS: Hold, press, pull, and tap the joints of all the fingers. If the sinus pain is very strong, wrap a rubber band around each finger joint one at a time. This will eventually allay the pain. Remove rubber bands within five to ten minutes, when a finger changes color, or if a finger is very uncomfortable. This should be avoided by people with poor circulation.

NAUSEA

When that Renaissance man, Dr. Jonathan Miller—director, actor, and medical doctor—developed a brilliant television series on the human body, he remarked that of all the ills one might endure, nausea was one of the most burdensome. The late Supreme Court Justice Benjamin Cardozo, who was prone to the nausea of motion sickness, might have agreed. One day when all the nine Supreme Court justices were out on a boat trip, Justice Cardozo got seasick. A fellow justice came over to him to ask if there was anything he could do. "Yes," replied the judge, "overrule the motion." Fortunately, the past offers many simple, natural answers to the difficult problem of nausea.

Ginger (*Zingiber offininalis*), which has been used as a medicinal herb for over two thousand years, originally came from tropical Asia. The Spanish loved the taste of ginger and brought it with them to the New World and established it as a crop in the West Indies. Scientists have recently confirmed what folk medicine has known forever: ginger is an outstanding aid in controlling nausea. DIRECTIONS: You can utilize ginger in any of its forms. Some village healers placed two drops of the essential oil on a sugar lump or combined the essential oil with a small amount of honey. Other healers grated fresh ginger into boiling water to make a restorative tea. Still others placed two to ten drops of ginger tincture in a glass of water and offered it to nauseous patients. Ginger now also comes in powdered capsules. Take one or two 200-mg ginger capsules before a journey as an antidote to motion sickness. For the nausea of pregnancy, limit intake to up to 1,000 mg or one gram per day.

The top side of the hand—especially the index finger and the thumb and the web between them—seems to have a direct connection to the stomach. DIRECTIONS: According to ancient Chinese writings, deep pressure with a metal comb or fingernails on this area will relieve the morning sickness of pregnancy.

Just the smell of mint refreshes our spirits and gives zest to food says the first-century Roman Pliny the Elder. To the ancients, mint had many uses. Both the Greeks and Romans used mint to scent their bathwater, and they strewed mint over the floor to keep away fleas. Sips of peppermint tea were known to ease all sorts of digestive problems including indigestion, flatulence, and nausea. As a result, peppermint was frequently used after most legendary Roman feasts.

In the Smoky Mountains, old-timers still take raspberry leaf tea to allay nausea. DIRECTIONS: Prepare a handful of fresh or dried raspberry leaves. Add to a cup of boiling water. Steep for five to ten minutes. Strain out leaves.

Sweet basil (*Ocium basilicum*) was often grown in Africa and used by African herbalists to relieve nausea and reduce severe vomiting. Sometimes the leaf was rubbed on the hands and across the stomach. Other times it was used as a tea. DIRECTIONS: Add a full cup of boiling water to a teaspoon of basil leaves. Steep, strain, and drink.

NOSEBLEEDS

Nosebleeds are generally more inconvenient than serious. Those who have them frequently should avoid drinking alcohol or eating foods containing salicylate, an anticoagulant component of aspirin. Among the foods to avoid are coffee, tea, almonds, cucumbers, pickles, green peppers, and tomatoes. Taking vitamin C will strengthen the walls of the nasal passages. Some people with high blood pressure may be inclined to nosebleeds.

All the Mediterranean countries used the aloe vera plant for first aid. Those who were prone to nosebleeds used the gel in the nose on a preventive basis. Small aloe vera plants are easily obtained in flower shops and are very hardy windowsill plants. DIRECTIONS: Break off one small leaf. Slit it open to expose its gel. Apply a thin dot of gel—or pure aloe vera ointment purchased from a health food store—in the nose to discourage excessive dryness. Repeat daily.

We can trace the use of cayenne pepper to stop bleeding as far back as the great Muslim physician Avicenna, who lived in the early Middle Ages. He and other ancient scholars of herbal medicine claimed that taking small amounts of cayenne every day can help with clotting in the case of nosebleeds. Add cayenne powder to salads, cooked foods, or add a pinch to any herbal tea.

Old Japanese medicine includes many finger pressure points to stop nosebleeds. DIRECTIONS: Gently blow the nose. With index finger and thumb squeeze the fleshy part of the nose for a few minutes. Keep head back to hinder the downward flow of blood. Or press the acupressure point on the back of the neck on either side of the vertebrae at the level of the ears. A second point is just beneath the base of the skull, on either side of the spine, just where the spine meets the skull. Press as needed.

We don't know whether the legendary pirate Captain Kidd buried his famous loot along the Hudson River or Long Island Sound, but we do know that he taught his crew to control nosebleeds by pinching the nose and applying ocean-cold compresses. DIRECTIONS: Pinch the nose closed for a moment, tilt the head back, then apply an ice pack to the bridge of the nose, neck, and cheek area. Also apply ice to the back of the neck.

The Native Americans always had distilled flowers and twigs from the witch hazel tree on hand to stop bleeding. To stop a nosebleed, Native Americans soaked moss in witch hazel and placed the mixture in the nose. DIRECTIONS: Witch hazel extract such as the reliable Dickinson brand is available in drugstores. Apply it with fingertip or cotton swab.

The Appalachian mountains were America's first frontier. Today, the descendants of the original settlers halt a nosebleed in the traditional way by inserting a coin under the nose between the upper lip and the gum and pressing hard on the coin. DIRECTIONS: Thoroughly wash the coin first.

The aerial parts of shepherd's purse (*Capsella bursa-pastorisis*) were used throughout Europe as a styptic to reduce bleeding. Centuries ago, they used a tincture of shepherd's purse on battlefield wounds. For nosebleeds, they soaked a tiny piece of cloth in the tincture and inserted it into the nostril. This is another herb to be avoided during pregnancy because it often brings on uterine contractions.

According to legend, Caesar's troops brought the Roman stinging nettle (*Urtica dioica*) into Britain with them because they thought they would need to flail themselves with nettles to keep warm. Nettle juice is an ancient medicine much used throughout the world as a cleansing spring tonic and a remedy to relieve gout (it helps to clear uric acid from the system). The leaves are very astringent. In ancient times, the leaves were crushed into a powder and inhaled as snuff to stop nosebleeds, or a tiny cloth was moistened with nettle juice and inserted into the nostrils.

RASHES

Skin eruptions are a symptom that something special has happened inside the body. Healers of the past were totally aware that it was better to find the cause of the rash than to push the rash back into the body. That's why many remedies insist on detoxification regimens, as well as healing of the rash itself. Homeopathic remedies are excellent for persistent rashes, but they require the diagnostic skill of a professional homeopath.

In natural healing of skin, the focus is on absorbing toxins within the skin and eliminating them. Native healers used clay packs to heal and eliminate rashes —especially hives, eczema, and psoriasis. DIRECTIONS: Buy either green clay, kaolin powder, or a neutral clay. Mix with water and apply to the rash. Leave on until the clay dries, flakes, and drops off. Wash the remaining clay residue off in warm, soothing water.

As the first horses moved from central Asia to Arabia and Egypt, then into ancient Greece and Rome, and finally with the Roman conquests to Europe, the cultivation of the oat soon followed. But people soon found that in addition to sustaining horses, oats are also a prime aid in healing skin rashes. DIRECTIONS: Apply a thin layer of cooked and slightly cooled oatmeal directly to the skin or encased in a soft cloth. Cooked oatmeal is messy, so if you are prone to hives or other rashes, or there is a baby in the house with diaper rash, you might prefer to buy some powdered suspended particles of oats sold under the name Aveeno. Unlike home-cooked cereal, Aveeno will dissolve instantly in water.

The Egyptian Copts are a remnant of early Christian communities that have not converted to Islam in the fourteen centuries since the Islamic invasion. In ancient times, the Copts used the rue plant to cure some skin problems. "Combine willow branches, fresh rue, grind it with wine," suggests one Coptic text. "Give it to the sick man to drink and they [sic] will get well." The Copts also used this remedy to cure "sick testicles." It is not surprising to see this reference to willow branches, as willow was widely used throughout the world to calm inflammation and fever. In the nineteenth century, scientists labored to produce a synthetic willow substance. The result? Aspirin.

Chamomile, one of the oldest of the garden plants, has been used for centuries as a versatile medicine. The Egyptians venerated it because it controlled ague (malarial fever). Smelling sweetly of apples, chamomile is one of the most familiar and used country remedies in the British Isles. The flowers are usually made into a sedative tea useful for calming anxiety and encouraging sleep. Chamomile also has extraordinary antiseptic abilities. Following is an old American country wash for the itchiness of eczema. DIRECTIONS: Prepare tea by steeping several tablespoons of the chamomile *flowers* in a cup of boiling water. Strain. Combine equal amounts of the tea and witch hazel extract and apply with cotton as necessary.

The Egyptian Copts made up an ointment based on aloe gel to treat a skin disease called Psora. "If you take a baked cucumber and grind it with aloe, add wine and anoint the affected parts with it, it will heal," one Coptic text suggested.

The pH of the cucumber plant is almost matched by the skin. Slices of cucumber can be applied to any skin irritation to provide cooling. Early American settlers applied raw cucumber directly to rashes. DIRECTIONS: Wash and peel one cucumber. You may place the slices of cucumber directly on the rash.

Knowing this ancient Chinese pressure point therapy may help control a rash. DIRECTIONS: Bend either your right or left arm tightly and place a finger at the end of the crease of the elbow, close to your body. Keep your finger in place. Open the arm and press the point on your relaxed arm.

Very few people realize that an itchy scalp usually appears as a reaction to shampoo. But in central European villages, residents use shampoos to solve the problem. DIRECTIONS: If there is only a *slightly* itchy scalp, wash the hair with coconut oil shampoo. If the scalp is *very* itchy use the following egg shampoo: Beat two or three raw eggs and slather them through the hair with the tips of your fingers. Rinse out with lukewarm water. Follow with a restorative and healing apple cider vinegar rinse (two tablespoons to a pint of water). Continue this shampoo for at least one month.

Flowers and stems of the pansy (*Viola tricolor*) or sweet violet (*Viola spp*) have been used medicinally since ancient times. The Greeks and Romans used the plant to sooth skin inflammation. Homer describes how the Athenians used violets to moderate anger, while Pliny writes that violets were employed to prevent dizziness and headache. They both used the sweet violet to treat severe eczema. DIRECTIONS: Mix fifteen drops of sweet violet tincture into a glass of water. Apply the water as a wash. The tincture can also be added to any neutral ointment base or petroleum jelly and applied as an ointment. For chronic skin disorders, make up a paste of powdered flowers and stems of pansy mixed with water and apply to skin sores and ulcers.

For many centuries, Europeans used the borage (*Borago offininalis*) plant and oil to control eczema. Their observations of its usefulness are nothing short of amazing. Current research reveals that eczema patients are in need of the nutrients found in borage. DIRECTIONS: Obtain borage capsules at health food stores. Follow package directions. Primrose oil and/or black currant seed oil contain similar unsaturated fatty acids that can be used instead of borage oil.

Often rashes are temporary and will disappear when the body is flushed with cleansing drinks and baths. Bavarian herbalist Sebastian Kneipp always recommended hayflower or oatstraw baths to soothe rashes. DIRECTIONS: Add a tablespoon of hayflower or oatstraw extract to warm bathwater and soak for a few minutes. Biokosma brand of Switzerland is an excellent hayflower bath extract. It can be purchased in health food stores.

SORE THROATS

Many sore throats get better after a few days, but some are the first indication that your immune system is running "on empty," and a cold is on the way. There are dozens of excellent, safe home remedies to relieve sore throat discomfort.

Before Hawaii was "discovered," the islands enjoyed a highly successful native medicine in which the local doctors had a rigorous fifteen-year apprenticeship. So what did these medicine men do for a sore throat or an inflamed tonsil? They squeezed the juice from fresh ginger root, warmed it up, and made their patients gargle vigorously with it. Could perfection be improved upon? It turns out that the answer is yes. When pineapple later became a major island crop, local healers discovered pineapple increased healing by getting rid of dead tissue in the throat. So they put the two remedies into a single gargle with a double whammy. This alternate gargle—first with *warm* ginger juice, then *cold* pineapple juice—is invaluable. DIRECTIONS: Steep a teaspoon of powdered ginger in half a cup of just-boiled water. Cool it to warm and add a quarter-teaspoon of honey and the juice of half a lemon. Gargle. Discard. Gargle with cool to cold pineapple juice. Repeat as necessary throughout the day.

Fresh beets that turn green? This Amish remedy for sore throat sounds like useful fun. DIRECTIONS: Gather together a dish towel, a safety pin, and two fresh beets. Grate the beets and place in about a four-inch wide strip in the middle of the towel. Fold the top of the towel down, then fold the bottom part of the towel up. This creates a three-part envelope with the beets in the middle. Place the towel around your neck *with the beet side to the throat.* Pin closely with the safety pin. When the beets change to a green color, discard that batch and start again with fresh beets and cloth. Repeat this action until you get a batch of beets that do not turn green! Be careful not to let the beets drip on fabrics—they stain.

Salt must be one of the oldest healing agents in the world—it is certainly used everywhere. This old remedy is one of the best to overcome a sore throat. DIRECTIONS: Add a teaspoon of salt to a glass of water and gargle with it as often as possible. To prevent a sore throat to begin with, people in India gargle every day to keep the throat clear of mucus. If you want to try their idea, add a pinch of salt plus a pinch of turmeric (on spice shelves of supermarkets) to a glass of warm water.

The early pioneers who settled America were hard-working people who resented any time lost to illness. That's why cayenne pepper became one of their favorite medicinal herbs. They added a pinch of cayenne to a glass of water, gargled vigorously, and in minutes the sore throat felt cauterized by the biting herb.

It took several hundred years for us to catch up and truly appreciate the purple coneflower—one of Native Americans' most useful antibacterial, antiviral, antifungal herbs. But within the last fifteen years, under its Latin name *Echinacea purpurea*, the coneflower has been sold as a valuable immune system stimulant that fights cold and flu. Echinacea is available as a tincture, tablet, or capsule in health food stores. DIRECTIONS: Add ten to sixteen drops of echinacea tincture to a glass of water. Sip about a quarter of the cup to help the immune system fight off whatever germ is causing your sore throat. Gargle with the rest and spit it out.

One of the best things about getting a sore throat when some of us were children was blackberry and/or raspberry jam gargle. DIRECTIONS: Add a teaspoon of either raspberry or blackberry jam to a glass of water and gargle. Repeat as often as necessary. Also drink a hot tea made of two tablespoons of the jam and a cup of boiling water.

If you are often prone to sore throats, try practicing this throat-strengthening gargle developed by ancient Indian yogis. DIRECTIONS: Use your favorite gargle (salt water is always dependable) and, while you are gargling, say the sounds OH, AY, MI, LI. This is hard to do, but persevere—it opens the throat.

Sauerkraut juice—the fermented juice of the cabbage plant—was used everywhere in Europe and in America by early settlers. It was gargled to heal a sore throat. DIRECTIONS: To make homemade sauerkraut, wash and dry scores of cabbage leaves, chop them up, and layer them in a crock. Sprinkle salt over each layer until the top is reached. Cover with a clean cloth and tightly weigh it down with a stone or heavy plates. Let it sit there for six weeks or more. Draw off the juice and gargle as needed.

Adam in Eden, published in 1657, was one of the most popular home remedy books of the seventeenth century. For a sore throat gargle, the book extols the value of marshmallow flowers boiled in water and sweetened with a small amount of honey. DIRECTIONS: Steep one teaspoon of marshmallow flowers in eight ounces of boiling water. Strain and add a dollop of honey. Sip as needed to ease the pain.

SPRAINS

Unexpected or abrupt movements during exercise—including the overstretching or overextension of muscles—sometimes cause tears called sprains and strains. After such an injury, the body releases many free radicals which should be fought with these oxidant scavengers: zinc, vitamins C, and E. Calcium intake is also important. The "B" family vitamins may help reduce swelling.

When people are injured, they sometimes use heat to ease the pain. Do not use heat, but instead use ice. All this was explained some century and a half ago by the renowned Bavarian herbalist Sebastian Kneipp as part of his water-based healing system. Today, all athletes immediately apply ice to injuries. It is *cold*, not heat, that contains potential swelling and restrains inflammation. Directions: Apply ice several times a day for the first twenty-four to thirty-six hours. Wrap it in a towel, place it on the injured area, and elevate whatever muscle got sprained. This is easily remembered with the word "RICE," which stands for Rest, Ice, Compression (use an elastic bandage when the ice is off the injured area), and Elevation. Alternating hot and cold treatment is best after the initial period has ended.

Russian villagers turned to one of their favorite healing foods—onions plus sugar—to heal a muscle sprain. Directions: Finely chop onions, sprinkle with granulated sugar, spread on a soft cloth, and apply to the sprain.

Throughout the centuries, Italians and later Italian-Americans employed apple cider vinegar to reduce the pain of strains and sprains. Directions: Soak a cloth in apple cider vinegar and apply to the area of sprain.

Hawaiian healers applied the pungent oil of *nuholani*, a substance we call eucalyptus, to sprains, backaches, sores, and even rheumatic pain. In a 1991 study, researchers discovered that a combination of either peppermint oil or eucalyptus oil could be useful to athletes for pain relief. DIRECTIONS: Soak a cloth in eucalyptus oil or peppermint oil or equal amounts of each mixed together and apply to sprain.

Fenugreek is probably one of the oldest known and cultivated medicinal plants. In some societies it was considered an aphrodisiac; in India and Pakistan it was used mainly to repel insects. And in all Arab lands, it was used internally and externally as a prime healer and anti-inflammatory agent. DIRECTIONS: To heal ankle sprains, Arabs grind a handful of fenugreek seeds and mix them with a tablespoon of powdered mustard seed and a pinch of salt, then apply and bandage the mixture to the injured area.

Turmeric is a common spice in Indian and Asian cooking and gives curry its distinctive color and aroma. But turmeric is also a powerful antioxidant that destroys dangerous free radicals. It is also a strong anti-inflammatory. Because of this last ability, it is one of the medicines used in the Ayurvedic system to control arthritis and reduce the inflammation in sprains. DIRECTIONS: To reduce swelling, combine a teaspoon or two of turmeric with hot water and apply the paste on the sprain.

Arnica is a traditional bruise and sprain remedy used by Native Americans and later as one of the keystone trauma and bruise homeopathic remedies. Homeopathic Arnica is available in health food stores and by mail. Directions: For trauma from injury and sprain, most people take four pills of Arnica (6x or 6c, or 9x or 9c), and—providing there are no abrasions on the skin—also apply Arnica ointment, or Arnica gel, directly to the sprain.

While we all know thyme as a popular spice, it has also been used widely by the ancient Greeks and Romans as an important topical medicine. Externally, the oil and the leaves act to bring blood to the surface of the skin. This action relieves pains, aches, and sprains. The oil, which can be obtained through mail order sources, may be patted on painful areas to reduce pain.

TOOTH SENSITIVITY

A throbbing, searing toothache has to be one of life's worst nightmares. Throughout history, each culture discovered plants and gums to numb, heal, and encase swollen, sensitive teeth. Nomadic Arab tribes, for instance, knew seventeen local plants to heal toothaches.

Egyptians drank anise tea to improve digestion, quiet headache pain, and mute coughs, and they chewed anise seeds to alleviate a toothache, according to the first-century physician Dioscorides. Directions: Bruise a handful of anise seeds and steep in boiling water for ten minutes. Strain out the seeds and drink the tea.

In *The Theatrum Botanium* of 1640, readers were advised to steep lavender flowers in boiling water to produce a sweet-smelling "garble" (gargle) against "the paines of the teeth." Lavender was also employed in British herbal medicine to preserve loose teeth. DIRECTIONS: Drop a handful of lavender flowers into a pot of boiling water. Let cool, strain out flowers, then gargle as needed.

Figs have often functioned as a nutritious food, helpful medicine, and poultice to draw out poisons since Biblical times. Toasted figs were favored for gum boils, while Italians often cut figs in half and placed them against a sore tooth to allay a toothache.

Calendula flowers were always a mainstay of European folk medicine. The Swiss, Belgians, and Dutch used calendula tea as a mouthwash to soothe sensitive gums. Today, calendula tea is also used after dental work to heal the gums. DIRECTIONS: Make calendula tea with one tablespoon of calendula flowers and one cup of boiling water. Steep for ten minutes. Discard the flowers. Swish through the mouth.

An old Russian remedy uses onions to mollify toothaches. It seems to be a crossover with ancient Chinese acupuncture. DIRECTIONS: Fry an onion and wrap it in a small cloth. If the toothache is on the right side of the mouth, put the cloth on the pulse of the right wrist. If the toothache is on the left side, place the cloth on the pulse of the left wrist. For front teeth, place the bag on the wrist just below the thumb joint of one or both hands.

Today marjoram (*Origanum majorana*) is chiefly known as a spice, particularly for Italian food. Theophrastus, a classical observer who lived between 372-287 B.C., says in his herbal that the Egyptians "chewed the leaves to soothe a toothache." The use of marjoram for toothache has persisted in the Near East. As recently as seventy-five years ago, Jews in Palestine placed a few drops of the oil of marjoram into painful cavities.

The Victorians loved to show cartoons of toothache victims—people with huge distended cheeks anxiously waiting outside a dentist's office. The swollen cheek was surely agony personified. But in Russia and the Balkans, the Slavs concocted a nettle remedy to reduce the swelling and claimed that it made the toothache disappear. DIRECTIONS: In a seasoned earthenware, glass, or nonaluminum pot, boil together a cupful of powdered nettle root and a pinch of saffron in a pint of fresh milk. As soon as the milk comes to a boil, reduce to a simmer. Immediately dip in a large clean cloth, wring it out, and apply the cloth directly over the swollen cheek. As soon as one compress cools, apply another hot one until the swelling is reduced.

In Spain, South America, Mexico, and the Caribbean Islands, residents have a unique cayenne pepper remedy for toothaches—one so strong that they claim it will make "the toothache become a thing of the past." DIRECTIONS: "Take one pod of cayenne pepper, cut off a little piece of the top, discard the seeds from the inside, fill it to the top with salt and pour a strong wine vinegar over the salt until it is full. Put this stuffed pepper pod into a very hot oven (the pod won't burn). When the vinegar comes to a boiling point, take it out. Take a cotton applicator, dip it into the inside of the pod and immediately apply this medicine to the aching tooth, and hold it until it cools off. Repeat several times."

Loose teeth were a problem in the last centuries, just as they are today. Old English herbalists had several approaches to this problem: "Take a quantity of blackberry roots, chop well and boil for half an hour with vinegar in a tightly covered casserole or pot. Wash teeth with this warm concoction three times a day. After three weeks of such washing there will not be any shaky teeth to be found....on the other hand, if this washing had not been done, most of the loose teeth would have fallen out."

Chamomile, a beloved French table tea, was often used for the nerves and digestion, as well as a healing poultice for toothache pain. DIRECTIONS: Dip one or more chamomile teabags into boiling water to release its volatile oils. Let cool enough to touch. Apply the teabag to the tooth, the gum, or the cheek to allay toothache pain. This can be repeated as often as necessary.

To the ancient Egyptians, the carob tree (*Ceraonia siliqua*) was "sweet pod pulp" so beloved that it shows up in a wall painting in a Theban tomb. A remedy "to treat a tooth which is eaten away where the gums begin" included equal parts of cumin, frankincense, and carob pulp ground to a powder and applied to a tooth.

VAGINAL INFECTIONS

The vaginal area is sensitive to changes in internal balance and thus prone to a variety of infections—all of which are loosely called vaginitis although each has a separate name. Common symptoms are itching or sometimes pain on urination. Other alerts can be an unusual discharge and a vaginal odor. Vaginitis ranges from common organisms that respond to simple changes of internal flora and acidity to more complex yeast infections and sexually transmitted diseases. These last will require professional phytomedicine (plant medicine) and/or antibiotic treatments. Untreated vaginitis can lead to tubal scarring and other serious conditions such as pelvic inflammatory disease, or PID. See your gynecologist or a holistic physician promptly for diagnosis and treatment.

Men and women live long lives in the mountains of the Caucasus. One of their ancient healing secrets is their use of yogurt, which acts as an internal antibacterial police force. To overcome simple vaginitis, these mountain women douche with diluted yogurt containing live organisms such as lactobacillis and also apply the yogurt directly to the vaginal area. Living organisms manufacture a digestive flora that resists many bacterial invasions. DIRECTIONS: Eat small amounts of natural lactobacillus yogurt several times a day. Every three days, douche with one cup of warm water into which you have mixed a half-teaspoon of *Lactobacillus acidophilus*. Each day, soak a tampon in yogurt and apply internally. Finish by patting the yogurt on the outer area of the vagina. Change tampons every three to six hours. Health food stores also carry Maxidolphilus or Megadolphius supplements which should be used according to directions.

Many old vaginitis remedies work by restoring the acid balance of the normal vagina. This is what the Japanese do when they utilize the versatile umeboshi plum to overcome vaginitis caused by *trichomonas*. Traditionally, the Japanese employ the umeboshi in two ways: as the active ingredient in a sitz bath and as the active ingredient on a cotton pad to be applied to the vagina.

DIRECTIONS: Prepare a moderately warm bath about six inches deep. Add one or two umeboshi plums to the water. Sit in this partial bath and let the essence of plum restore the acidity to your vagina. In addition, steep a third umeboshi plum in a pint of water. Strain out the plum then soak either a tampon or a sterilized cotton pad in the plum water. Wear the tampon internally or apply the cotton pad directly to the outer vaginal area.

Common kitchen substances are often very effective medicine. In Europe, apple cider vinegar and water have been a dependable old remedy for the painful, itching discharge caused by *Trichomonas vaginalis*. One, but certainly not the only cause of this discharge, is a forgotten tampon. DIRECTIONS: Once the tampon is out, it is simple to restore the normal pH balance by douching several times a day with diluted apple cider vinegar. Often the problem discharge simply vanishes and never returns. The ancient Greeks also recommended drinking apple cider vinegar mixed with honey and water, a restorative they called "oxymel." To make, thoroughly mix a tablespoon each of pure honey and apple cider vinegar. Add to a six- to eight-ounce glass of pure water. Drink several times a day. This solution can also be made up in advance and stored in the refrigerator.

There are five basic types of traditional healers in Africa. One functions very much like a western physician, except that he offers only plants as medicine. And although *Echinacea purpurea* was originally grown in North America, African healers have prescribed it since it was brought to parts of Africa about 150 years ago. They frequently suggest a fluid extract of echinacea either as an ointment, a poultice, or a vaginal insert to cure *trichomonas*.

Today we know that echinacea can inhibit the production of certain bacteria, and clinical studies show that it inhibits activity of *Trichomonas vaginalis.*

Modern research shows that the calendula plant is an effective antifungal. Calendula oil has been used for centuries throughout Europe for vaginitis caused by a yeast infection. Since this oil might be hard to obtain, here is an easy cold-infusion recipe. DIRECTIONS: Steep a handful of fresh or dried calendula flowers in about a pint of olive, sesame, or safflower oil in a jar in the sun for seven days. Then drain out the flowers and use the calendula-infused oil. Wash the vaginal area with this oil and add a tablespoon or two to douche water.

When Captain Cook discovered the aborigines using tea tree oil (*Melaleuca alternifolia*) in the 1700s, he could hardly have envisioned that one of its best uses would be against a number of routine vaginal problems such as *Candida albicans* and *trichomonas*. Tea tree oil is a potent antiseptic that is said not to irritate the vaginal membranes. It should be diluted before use. DIRECTIONS: Buy products such as Desert Essence tea tree oil, which has a twenty percent concentration of the oil. To prepare a douche: Dilute the oil by adding one teaspoon of tea tree oil to a pint of warm water. Then gently wash the entire outer vaginal area with soap and water. Dry thoroughly. Wash the area with the diluted tea tree oil and also use as a douche. Such douches are very successful and may be the only treatment needed. For a tampon treatment, use one percent tea tree oil to wash the area thoroughly. Put five drops of the twenty percent tea tree oil on the tampon and insert for four to six hours. Current plant experts recommend this treatment be continued for up to two months, although you should check with your doctor first. It is also quite effective to combine diluted tea tree oil with calendula oil. Shape a suppository using cocoa butter plus each of the oils. Place in the freezer to harden. When inserted, the cocoa butter melts at body temperature and releases the oils so that they can heal the area. Wear a sanitary napkin to avoid staining clothes.

Garlic! It is one of the oldest and most reliable anti-infection cures used by mankind—and womankind. For vaginal infections you can use garlic systemically and topically. DIRECTIONS: Eat plenty of fresh garlic. One delicious way is to make a huge salad of finely cut beefsteak tomatoes, red onions, lemon juice, and fresh, crushed garlic cloves (that's four anti-infection food medicines!) plus a small amount of olive oil. For suppositories of garlic, whittle a garlic clove into a suppository shape. Enclose the garlic in a piece of sterile gauze with some clean new string wrapped around it and hanging out. The gauze prevents burning; the string helps you to withdraw the suppository. Before inserting, rub oil over the gauze. Withdraw and reinsert a fresh suppository every few hours. Don't forget to take the old suppositories out.

Ladies Mantle was one of the most popular wound herbs on the battlefields of the fifteenth and sixteenth century. In that period, they also used this plant in an ointment to overcome vaginal itching of any kind. The plant is a uterine stimulator, so do not use it during pregnancy. DIRECTIONS: Combine an ounce of rosewater, two ounces of any neutral ointment base or petroleum jelly, and twenty drops of the tincture of Ladies Mantle. Apply to the vaginal area each morning and evening.

VISION PROBLEMS

Thousands of years ago, knowledgeable doctors from China and India invented powerful eye muscle exercises to insure good sight. While the ancient Chinese mainly used simple touch points, the Indians devised a series of easy eye movements. The worldwide followers of these time-honored exercises maintained strong eyesight into old age.

Since it is impossible to maintain good vision with dry eyes, the canny Scots invented a tear-inducer compress. DIRECTIONS: Soak a soft cloth in warm to nearly-hot water. Wring out the cloth and apply it over the eyes. The warmth unclogs the tear ducts and coaxes the eyes to lubricate naturally.

To help overcome dry eyes and increase circulation in the sluggish area around the eyes, Chinese doctors created this quick daily, self-help eye massage. DIRECTIONS: Each day, with the pad of the index finger or the knuckle of the thumb, press the eye muscle points above and below the eye socket area. Then with pads of thumbs, press closed eyelids for ten seconds.

Venerable Ayurvedic doctors in India designed a series of easy eye movements called mudras. Practiced daily, Vedic practitioners believe mudras help individuals to see more clearly and read from great distances. They also maintain that mudras improve one's powers of memory and concentration. DIRECTIONS:

1. Stare at the tip of your nose.
2. Using a finger or a pencil, focus your eyes on something near.

3. Focus your eyes on the far horizon.
4. Place an open book or a printed notice several feet from you. Gradually, over time, increase the distance so that you can read it from far away. After a time, many people can read a notice from the back of a large room.
5. With both eyes, look up to the far right. Look diagonally down to the far left.
6. With both eyes, look up to the far left. Look diagonally down to the far right.

Vedic doctors in India use this age-old water bath to prevent cataracts. The use of saliva may surprise you, but Deeprak Chopra, M. D., a modern Vedic doctor and lecturer, explains that saliva contains an enzyme that digests the protein of which cataracts are made. He believes this wash has helped untold generations of Indians avoid cataracts. But because saliva can contain bacteria, you may wish to discuss the remedy with your personal physician before you try it. DIRECTIONS: Thoroughly scrub and rinse mouth, teeth, and gums. Prepare a clean six- to eight-ounce glass of water, then spit a tablespoon's-worth of saliva into the glass of water. Mix the saliva and water, then wash your eyes with the mixture.

Indian yogis practice a several-thousand-year-old series of body and eye exercises called hatha yoga. The following circular eye movement from this discipline is designed to keep the eye muscles strong and supple. Be patient in learning this exercise, for initially the movement is jerky. After practice, the maneuver will become even and steady. DIRECTIONS: Roll both your eyes in an upward half circle from left to right. Next, roll both your eyes in an upward half-circle from right to left. Then make a downward half-circle from left to right, then right to left. With a week to several weeks, you can combine all the half-circles into one smooth, full circle motion. Repeat at least once a day.

WARTS

Seventy-five percent of the population has warts at some time or other. Most occur on young children and young adults and can range from the infinitesimal to the size of a pea. They can be flat or raised, wet or dry. Warts are viral and spread by picking and touching. If you are plagued by continuous crops of warts, consider bolstering the immune system with careful vitamin supplementation. Vitamin C is especially important. Genital warts are sometimes indicators of a more serious condition and should be attended to by a physician. There are also several excellent genital wart protocols with phytomedicines (plant medicines) used by physicians. The following are old folk remedies from various continents and countries. Some work better if the wart is filed down with an emery board after application. Throw away the board after each filing to avoid contagion.

An application of fresh garlic is an old European folk remedy for getting rid of common skin warts. DIRECTIONS: Crush some fresh garlic or use garlic oil. Apply to the wart and cover with a bandaid for a day. A blister will form. The wart will fall off in about a week.

Goldenseal powder is a potent antiviral much used by early settlers of America. DIRECTIONS: Mix the powder with enough water to make a paste and apply directly to the wart. You may also take goldenseal capsules to strengthen the immune system. Do not use goldenseal if pregnant, since it is a uterine stimulant.

Tea tree oil is an invaluable antiseptic that was first discovered by Australian aborigines. It is useful for most warts. DIRECTIONS: Each day, apply with a cotton applicator. The oil is available in most health food stores and by mail order. (See Appendix I.)

Spongy warts and other fungus growths respond to topical applications of tincture of thuja, which is made by collecting young shoots of yellow cedar in May or June before the flowers emerge. DIRECTIONS: Once a day, apply with a cotton swab, but avoid contact with the surrounding skin. The tincture is available from special mail order services. (See Appendix I.)

Wherever the aloe vera plant grows in Asia, the Near East, or the Caribbean, the gel has been used to vanquish warts. DIRECTIONS: Cut off a leaf and slit it open to reveal its gel. Scrape the gel and apply it directly to the wart several times a day.

Dandelion "milk" or juice is a traditional English wart remedy. DIRECTIONS: Slice the dandelion's stem and pour the milky juice on the wart.

To rid themselves of warts, the Amish people have a tradition of rubbing the wart with peelings from fresh potatoes.

Older Latvians follow ancient tradition when they use the celandine plant as a medicine. The 1819 American *Family Receipt Book* recommends using the fresh juice of the celandine plant to eliminate unsightly warts. DIRECTIONS: Apply the juice or a well-diluted tincture to the wart with a cotton-tipped swab.

There is an old English mullein remedy for warts that have a rough texture. DIRECTIONS: Apply the juice or the powder of the mullein root to the wart once a day until the wart is reduced and disappears.

Thyme oil is one of nature's best antiseptics and was often used throughout Europe to overcome warts. DIRECTIONS: Apply nightly. If no oil is available, apply a bruised thyme leaf each night. Attach with a bandaid.

WRINKLES/ AGING PROBLEMS

Everyone wants to look as young as they feel. But despite our good intentions, the skin loses moisture, elasticity, and internal cell support as we age. As a result, our precious skin becomes thirstier and thinner and shows more creases. Our exposure to the sun, the food we eat, and the care we give to the skin all influence the lines and wrinkles we get. As we age, there is more need to replace fast-dwindling skin cells. This is accomplished with food and exercise. The right foods slow down loss of elasticity, while vigorous exercise increases blood circulation that supplies proper nutrients to the skin. But staying youthful goes beyond food and exercise and includes the commitment to continuously expand one's mind and spirit.

When the world was much younger, the Do-In monks of China created a daily self-massage to keep healthy, vigorous, and long-lived. The monks believed the *Shen Men* point, a spot under the little finger at the edge of the palm side of the wrist, is the "Door of the Spirit." In Do-In, they believe one can slow down the aging process, strengthen the immune system, and promote smooth circulation of *Chi* (energy) by massaging and pressing the *Shen Men* point each day.

Fresh or dried powder of cayenne has many ancient medicinal uses. Asians and Mexican Indians believe that a daily pinch of the pepper in food or in hot tea will postpone many aging problems, including mental deterioration.

Long ago, French beauties used fennel seed "packs" to offset aging-skin problems. DIRECTIONS: Mash a handful of fennel seeds and steep in boiling water. Strain out the seeds, add to two tablespoons of yogurt, and one of honey. Apply as a mask to the face for thirty minutes. Rinse off.

The 1657 herbal *Adam In Eden* offers a highly regarded ointment for sunburn and wrinkles. "As divers Ladies, Gentlewomen and she Citizens whether wives or widows know well enough, an oynment made of the leaves of cowslips and hogs grease, healeth wounds, and taketh away spots, wrinkles and sunburnings, as so doth the distill water of the flowers." Cowslip (*Primula veris*) is a honey-scented, bright yellow flower that was also much favored by gypsies who used it to allay nervousness and to induce sleep when pain was present. DIRECTIONS: Add a handful of the flowers to a pint of boiling water. Simmer for ten minutes to make a tea and use the tea as a face wash. Or simmer a handful of flowers in half a cup of cocoa butter. Strain out flowers. Apply as antiwrinkle ointment to the face before bed.

Lemon balm, or Melissa, tea has been believed to insure long life and protect against senility since medieval times. Centuries ago, under the Klosterfrau label, Carmelite nuns prepared an elixir, Melisana, that is still sold in Germany, France, and Belgium. Directions: To prevent wrinkles, pour one cup of boiling water over one tablespoon of dried lemon balm leaves and steep. Drink once a day. Or eat raw lemon balm leaves everyday in your salad.

Chinese healers first described "Youth Breath," or Prana, in the sixth century B.C. Indian and Chinese monks used Prana breathing techniques to extend their lives. Chances are, they also eased the visible effects of aging. Directions: Keep in mind three concepts: relaxation, comfort, and awareness of breath. Breathe in through your nose, then fill first your diaphragm, then your upper respiratory system. The breaths you take will then "feed your entire system." Place the palms of your hands over your ears with your fingers entwined on your neck. Press the fingers gently together. As you breathe in and out, gently make believe you are chewing. Swallow. Keep on breathing as you then rub your tongue over your gums, teeth, and palate. Swallow gently. With your hands still on your ears and neck, and while still gently breathing, softly turn your head and shoulders to the right and left. Keep on breathing gently. Rub your palms together to warm them up and gently massage your neck and shoulders, your sides, and your abdomen. Keep on softly breathing in and out. Tighten your fists and gently, comfortably, extend your arms in and out. Put your fists on your chest and rotate your shoulders backwards. Extend your arms and create fists. Then open your hands, palms upwards. Bring the open palms to your face. Relax all your muscles and joints. Breathe in and out slowly and smoothly.

In the Caribbean Islands many women maintain glorious, lustrous youthful skin by eating a piece of avocado each day and massaging some avocado pulp into their skin every morning and evening.

The women of Argentina are known for their attractive and soft skin. To keep wrinkles away, they apply a honey facial several times a week. They let the honey dry for five to ten minutes, then gently rinse it off. Honey may be mixed with other foods such as avocado, apple cider vinegar, or lemon juice for a variation of masks.

This ancient Egyptian recipe found on a papyrus is an ointment "... Of making an old man into a young man."

> Collect a quantity of fenugreek about two sacks full, then you shall break them up and lie (them) in the sun. When they are completely dry, you shall thresh them like you would thresh barley. Then you must winnow it down to the last pod. Measure and sift, divide it into two portions, one consisting of the seeds, the other of the pod, ... Then you place them in water, the two portions have been combined. Knead it into a dough. Place it a new (clean) pot on the fire and boil it for a long time. You will recognize it when it is done, when the water has evaporated and they dry up until they are as dry as straw with no

moisture at all. (Then) take them away from the fire. When they have cooled, place them in a pot and wash them in the river. Wash them thoroughly. You will know when they are washed enough when you taste the water in the pot and there is no bitter taste left. Then you shall leave them in the sun spread out on a piece of laundryman's cloth. When they are dry, you shall grind them on the millstone until they have been reduced to small pieces. Then you shall steep them in water and make them into a soft dough. Then you shall place them in a vessel on the fire and cook them for a long time. You will know then they are done when the pellets of oil rise to the surface. All the time you must skim the oil which has risen with a spoon. Place it in the jar whose inner surface has been plastered with clay, smooth and thick. Skim the oil and strain it into the jar through a cloth. Then you shall place it in a jar of stone and use it as an unguent. It is a remedy for illness in the head. When the body is rubbed with it, the skin is left beautiful without any blemishes. *It is a million times efficient.*

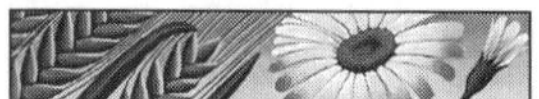 Panax ginseng is an ancient Chinese herb mentioned over two thousand years ago in the Chinese pharmacopeia, *Shen Nung Pen Ts'ao.* Panax means panacea, and this root has been used and continues to be used to overcome general problems of aging, including recovery from an illness, low energy levels, impotence, hot flashes, and heat in general. Chinese, Korean, and Russian studies show ginseng enhances memory. DIRECTIONS: Ginseng is available as a capsule, powder, and extract at health food stores. Follow package directions.

APPENDIX I
MAIL-ORDER SOURCES

NATIONAL MAIL-ORDER CATALOGS

Caswell-Massey
(800) 326-0500
Old-fashioned cosmetic and healing remedies.

East Earth Trade Winds
P.O. Box 493151
1620 E. Cypress Avenue #8
Redding, CA 96049-3151
(800) 258-6878
Traditional Chinese herbs and herb products.

Maharishi Ayur-Ved Products
P.O. Box 49667
Colorado Springs, CO 80949-9667
(800) 255-8332
Authentic Ayurvedic health and beauty products.

Himalayan Institute
RR 1 Box 400
Honesdale, PA 18431
(800) 822-4547
Ayurvedic Neti Pot to cleanse nasal passages.

The Heritage Store
P.O. Box 444-W
Virginia Beach, VA 23458-0444
(800) 862-2923
Pure castor oil and castor oil packs, Abra Salt cellular detox bath, oils, and hundreds of other exceptional healing items.

Walnut Acres Organic Farms
Penns Creek, PA 17862
(800) 433-3998
Full-spectrum incandescent bulbs that duplicate the characteristics of natural sunlight, homeopathic medicine chest, and hundreds of organic food produxts.

Green Mountain Mercantile
P.O. Box 3100
Manchester Center, VT 05255
(802) 362-2575
Flax-seed eye pillow for tired eyes.

Vitamin Shoppe
4700 Westside Avenue
North Bergen, NJ 07047
(800) 223-1216
Vitamins, homeopathic remedies, and herbs.

Self Care Catalog
5850 Shellmound Street
Emeryville, CA 94608-1901
(800) 345-3371
Every backup item for health care including many pain relief items that you never imagined—several relating to acupressure.

The Body Shop
45 Horschild Road
Cedar Knolls, NJ 07927-2014
(800) 541-2535
Hundreds of body-cleansing items including "rough" mitts to purify the skin.

HERBAL RESOURCES

Blake Natural Herbs and Spices
505 N. Railroad
Ellensburg, WA 98926
(800) 932-HERB
Organic and non-radiated herbs and spices.

Blessed Herbs
Rte. 5, Box 1042
Ava, MO 65608
(417) 683-5721
Wildcrafted and organic dried herbs.

Dry Creek Herb Farm
13035 Dry Creek Road
Auburn, CA 95602
(916) 878-2441
Organically grown herbs.

Native Essences
(800) 358-0513 information
(800) 234-3425 credit card orders
Old Indian good health herbal formula discovered by nurse Rene Caisse, available in dry or tincture form.

Minister of Supply
P.O. Box 1175
Mill Valley, CA 94942
Wide variety of blended and Japanese teas.

Terra Firma Botanicals
126 Sutherlin La.
Eugene, OR 95405
Wildcrafted and other organic herbal products, fresh and dried herbal extracts, flower oils, skin salves, massage oils.

Weleda, Inc.
P.O. Box 769
Spring Valley, NY 10977
(800) 241-1030
Calendula and other organic healing products, many for children

ORGANIC ESSENTIAL OILS SUPPLIERS

Ayesha Products, Inc.
Langhorne, PA 19047
(800) 440-4687

Inner Essence
212 E. Crest Drive
Eugene, OR 97405
(800) 821-3029

Oshadhi Essential Oils
P.O. Box 824
Rogers, AR 72757
(501) 636-0579

APPENDIX II
NATURAL HEALTH PRACTITIONERS ORGANIZATIONS

Ayurvedic Institute
11311 Menaul NE Suite A
Albuquerque, NM 87112
(505) 291-9698

American Association of
Naturopathic Physicians
2366 Eastlake Avenue East
Suite 322
Seattle WA

American Herbalists Guild
P.O. Box 4101 Lake Boone Trail
Suite 201
Raleigh, NC 27607
(919) 787-5181

American School of Ayurvedic
Sciences
10025 NE 4th Street
Bellevue, WA 98004
(206) 453-8022

American Association of
Acupuncture and Oriental
Medicine
433 Front Street
Catasauqua, PA 18032
(610) 433-2448

ABOUT THE AUTHOR

Dian Dincin Buchman is an expert in the field of natural health and natural medicine. She comes from a line of pioneers in natural medicine. Her grandmother, a Rumanian herbalist, acquired much healing knowledge from gypsies. Her father was a doctor who practiced drugless therapy. She has maintained her own and her family's good health for many years using natural, non-drug alternative therapies.

A resident of New York City, Buchman has a Ph.D. in Health Science. She also writes for *Health Quarterly* and lectures on the college circuit.

She is also the author of: *Herbal Medicine*, *The ABC's of Natural Beauty*, *The Complete Herbal Guide to Natural Health and Beauty*, and *The Complete Book of Water Therapy*.